cirencester
college
a beacon college

Principles and Prac...
in t...
Lifelong Learn...

D0588979

Cirenc... ...eg
Libra...

Principles and Practice of Assessment in the Lifelong Learning Sector

Second edition

Ann Gravells

First published in 2009 by Learning Matters Ltd
Reprinted in 2009
Reprinted in 2010

Second edition published in 2011
Reprinted in 2012

British Library Cataloguing in Publication Data
A CIP record for this book is available from the British Library.

ISBN: 978 0 85725 260 9

This book is available in the following ebook formats:
Adobe ebook ISBN: 978 0 85725 262 3
EPUB ebook ISBN: 978 0 85725 261 6
Kindle ISBN: 978 0 85725 263 0

The right of Ann Gravells to be identified as the Author of this work has been asserted by her in accordance with the Copyright, Design and Patents Act 1988.

Cover design by Topics – The Creative Partnership
Project management by Deer Park Productions, Tavistock, Devon
Typeset by Pantek Arts Ltd, Maidstone, Kent
Printed and bound in Great Britain by the MPG Books Group

Learning Matters
An imprint of SAGE Publications Ltd
1 Oliver's Yard
55 City Road
London EC1Y 1SP

SAGE Publications Inc.
2455 Teller Road
Thousand Oaks, California 91320

SAGE Publications India Pvt Ltd
B 1/1 1 Mohan Cooperative Industrial Area
Mathura Road
New Delhi 110 044

SAGE Publications Asia-Pacific Pte Ltd
3 Church Street
#10–04 Samsung Hub
Singapore 049483

MIX
Paper from
responsible sources
FSC® C018575

CONTENTS

ACKNOWLEDGEMENTS

The author would like to thank the following for their support and encouragement while writing this book.

Sharron Carlill
Jennifer Clark
Peter Frankish
Rosie Frankish
Tom Frankish
Bob Gravells
Julia Morris
Susan Simpson
Amy Thornton
Joan Willison

The students and staff of the teacher/training department at Bishop Burton College.

Reviewers of the first edition who have taken the time to give valuable feedback.

Ann Gravells is a lecturer in teacher training at Bishop Burton College in East Yorkshire. She has been teaching since 1983.

She is a consultant to City & Guilds for various projects as well as externally verifying the City & Guilds teacher training qualifications.

Ann holds a Masters in Educational Management, a PGCE, a Degree in Education, and a City & Guilds Medal of Excellence for teaching.

Ann is a Fellow of the Institute for Learning and holds QTLS status.

She is the author of:

- *Preparing to Teach in the Lifelong Learning Sector;*
- *Passing PTLLS Assessments;*
- *Principles and Practice of Assessment in the Lifelong Learning Sector;*
- *Delivering Employability Skills in the Lifelong Learning Sector.*

She is co-author of:

- *Planning and Enabling Learning in the Lifelong Learning Sector;*
- *Equality and Diversity in the Lifelong Learning Sector.*

She has edited:

- *Study Skills for PTLLS.*

The author welcomes any comments from readers; please contact her via her website.

Website – **www.anngravells.co.uk**

In this chapter you will learn about:

- the structure of the book and how to use it;
- Lifelong Learning professional teaching standards;
- Learning and Development Assessor Units.

The structure of the book and how to use it

This book has been specifically written for teachers and assessors who are working towards the Certificate in Teaching in the Lifelong Learning Sector (CTLLS) and/or the Learning and Development Assessor Units. Principles and Practice of Assessment is a core unit of the CTLLS qualification; however, the content is applicable to anyone requiring further information to assist their role as an assessor, or for continuing professional development (CPD).

The book is structured in chapters which relate to the content of the units. You can work logically through the book or just look up relevant aspects within the chapters. The contents build upon the information in the companion books by Gravells (2011) *Preparing to Teach in the Lifelong Learning Sector*, and Gravells and Simpson (2010) *Planning and Enabling Learning in the Lifelong Learning Sector*.

There are activities to enable you to think about how you assess, examples to help you understand the subject of assessment, and extension activities to stretch and challenge your learning further.

At the end of each chapter is a reference and further information list, enabling you to research relevant topics further, by using textbooks, publications and/or the internet.

Each chapter is cross-referenced to the new overarching professional standards for teachers, tutors and trainers in the Lifelong Learning Sector, and the Learning and Development Assessor Units.

Chapter 7 contains sample documents and pro-formas that you might wish to use when assessing. However, do check with your organisation in case they have particular documents they require you to use.

The appendices contain the qualification criteria for the CTLLS standards at levels 3 and 4, the Learning and Development standards at level 3, and an assessor checklist.

The index will help you to quickly locate useful topics.

Lifelong Learning professional teaching standards

In September 2007 professional standards came into effect for all new teachers in the Lifelong Learning Sector who teach or assess on government-funded programmes in England. See the weblinks at the end of the chapter for Northern Ireland, Scotland and Wales.

The full standards encompass six domains.

A Professional Values and Practice.

B Learning and Teaching.

C Specialist Learning and Teaching.

D Planning for Learning.

E Assessment for Learning.

F Access and Progression.

As you progress through the teaching qualifications, you will need to meet all the relevant criteria relating to the scope, knowledge and practice required in your job role (referenced by: S for *scope*, K for *knowledge* or P for *practice* within the chapters).

Levels

The content of the qualification's learning outcomes is the same at both level 3 and level 4; the difference in level is expressed in the amount of work you will be required to submit for the assessment criteria. For example, if you are taking level 3 you will *explain* how or why you do something, whereas at level 4 you will *analyse* how or why you do it. If you are working towards level 4 you will need to carry out relevant research, reference your work to theorists and use an academic style of writing.

The qualifications have been developed based upon the Qualifications and Credit Framework (QCF) model, which has mandatory and optional units at different levels, and with different credit values. The units and credits can be built up to form relevant qualifications over time. Principles and Practice of Assessment is a three-credit unit, available at levels 3 and 4, and can be found in Appendix 1.

The QCF has nine levels: entry, plus 1 to 8. The framework helps learners compare the requirements at each level and identify a suitable progression route.

Each unit has a credit value which represents ten hours, showing how much time it takes to complete a unit; for example, a three-credit unit would be 30 hours. There are three sizes of qualifications:

- awards (1 to 12 credits);
- certificates (13 to 36 credits);
- diplomas (37 credits or more).

Further information regarding qualifications and levels can be found at the direct.gov website via the internet shortcut **http://tinyurl.com/66ftqx**.

There are three teaching qualifications which fit into the new structure.

- Award in Preparing to Teach in the Lifelong Learning Sector (PTLLS) – a threshold licence to teach, at levels 3 and 4;

- Certificate in Teaching in the Lifelong Learning Sector (CTLLS) at levels 3 and 4, for *associate teachers*.

- Diploma in Teaching in the Lifelong Learning Sector (DTLLS) at level 5 and above, for *full teachers*.

If you are an *associate teacher*, you will need to take PTLLS and CTLLS. If you are a *full teacher* you will need to take PTLLS and DTLLS.

For the purpose of the teaching regulations, the Institute for Learning (IfL) definitions of *associate* and *full* teacher apply whether you are working on a full time, part time, fractional, fixed term, temporary or agency basis:

Associate Teaching role means a teaching role that carries significantly less than the full range of teaching responsibilities and does not require the teacher to demonstrate an extensive range of knowledge, understanding and application of curriculum innovation or curriculum delivery strategies.

Full Teaching role means a teaching role that carries the full range of teaching responsibilities and requires the teacher to demonstrate an extensive range of knowledge, understanding and application of curriculum innovation or curriculum delivery strategies.

Institute for Learning – internet shortcut: http://tiny.cc/dnx4e

All teachers must register with the IfL, the professional body for teachers, trainers, tutors and trainee teachers in the Learning and Skills Sector, and maintain their continuing professional development (CPD). Once registered, you must abide by their Code of Professional Practice; further details can be found via their website at **www.ifl.ac.uk**.

The Principles and Practice of Assessment unit can be taken independently from any of the teaching qualifications, as evidence towards CPD.

Registering with the IfL, gaining the relevant qualification, and maintaining your CPD, will enable you to apply for your teaching status. This will be either: Associate Teacher Learning and Skills (ATLS) for associate teachers, or Qualified Teacher Learning and Skills (QTLS) for full teachers. This is a requirement under the Further Education Teachers' Qualifications (England) Regulations (2007).

Learning and Development Assessor Units

These units have replaced the Learning and Development A1 and A2 assessor units (previously known as D32/33). They form part of the Training, Assessment and Quality Assurance (TAQA) suite of qualifications for England, Wales and

Northern Ireland; separate standards will be available in Scotland. They are suitable for anyone assessing occupational competence in any type of work environment, and/or vocational skills, knowledge and understanding in any other environment. The first unit is a theory unit (knowledge-based) and the others are practical units (performance-based).

There are three units which are only available at level 3 (see Appendices 2, 3 and 4).

1. Understanding the Principles and Practices of Assessment (3 credits). This is a knowledge-based unit for new and existing assessors or anyone who wishes to know about the theory of assessment. You do not need to carry out any assessment activities with learners to achieve this unit.

2. Assess Occupational Competence in the Work Environment (6 credits). This is a practical unit for anyone who assesses in the work environment using methods such as discussions, observations, questions and examining products of work. It doesn't have to be towards a qualification, it can be to assess on-the-job training of employees or volunteers.

3. Assess Vocational Skills, Knowledge and Understanding (6 credits). This is a practical unit for anyone who assesses in any other environment using methods such as assignments, case studies, projects, questions, simulations and tests.

As the first unit is purely knowledge-based, it can be taken prior to, or alongside, either the second or third unit. Unit 1 is ideal for anyone wanting to know what it's like to be an assessor, before actually assessing. To achieve unit 2 and/or 3, you will need to assess two learners on two occasions, using at least two methods (for each unit). You may need to have your decisions countersigned by another qualified assessor in your subject area.

Units 1 and 2 will lead to the Award in Assessing Competence in the Work Environment; Units 1 and 3 will lead to the Award in Assessing Vocationally Related Achievement. If all three units are achieved this will lead to the Certificate in Assessing Vocational Achievement. The units can be achieved in any order.

Although the first unit has a similar title to the CTLLS unit, the content is slightly different. However, evidence from one unit may be used towards achievement of other units if it is applicable. This textbook covers the requirements of all the units; however, you will need to ascertain which units are appropriate to your job role before embarking upon an appropriate route to becoming a qualified assessor.

Summary

In this chapter you have learnt about:

- the structure of the book and how to use it;
- Lifelong Learning professional teaching standards;
- Learning and Development Assessor Units.

Theory focus

References and further information

Gravells, A. (2011) *Preparing to Teach in the Lifelong Learning Sector* (4th edn). Exeter: Learning Matters.

Gravells, A. and Simpson, S (2010) *Planning and Enabling Learning in the Lifelong Learning Sector* (2nd edition). Exeter: Learning Matters.

LLUK (2006) *New Overarching Professional Standards for Teachers, Tutors and Trainers in the Lifelong Learning Sector*. London: Skills for Business.

Websites

Further Education Teachers' Qualifications (England) Regulations (2007) – **www.legislation.gov.uk/si/si2007/2264/contents/made**

Further Education Teacher's Qualification (Wales) – **http://tiny.cc/08uho**

Institute for Learning – **www.ifl.ac.uk**

Professional Standards for Lecturers in Scotland – **http://tiny.cc/3w9jg**

Teaching Qualifications for Northern Ireland – **http://tiny.cc/2bexb**

The Learning and Skills Improvement Service – **www.isis.org.uk**

1 KEY CONCEPTS AND PRINCIPLES OF ASSESSMENT

Introduction

In this chapter you will learn about:

- concepts and principles of assessment;

- the assessment cycle;

- roles and responsibilities of an assessor;

- communicating with others.

There are activities and examples to help you reflect on the above which will assist your understanding of the key concepts and principles of assessment. At the end of each section is an extension activity to stretch and challenge your learning further.

This chapter contributes towards the following: scope (S), knowledge (K) and practice (P) aspects of the professional standards (A–F domains) for teachers, tutors and trainers in the Lifelong Learning Sector.

AS1, AS2, AS5;
AK1.1, AK4.1, AK5.1, AK5.2, AK6.1, AK6.2, AK7.1, AK7.2;
AP1.1, AP4.1, AP5.1, AP5.2, AP6.1, AP7.1;
BS1, BS2, BS3, BS4;
BK1.1, BK1.3, BK2.2, BK2.3, BK2.7, BK3.5, BK4.1;
BP1.3, BP2.7, BP3.1, BP3.5, BP4.1;
CS2;
CP1.1, CP2.1;
DK2.1;
ES1, ES2, ES3, ES5;
EK1.1, EK2.2, EK2.3, EK2.4, EK3.2, EK5.1, EK5.2, EK5.3;
EP2.2, EP2.4, EP5.1, EP5.5;
FS2;
FK2.1, FK4.2;
FP2.1, FP4.2.

This chapter contributes towards the following Learning and Development Assessor Units:

Unit 1: 1.1, 1.2, 1.3, 1.4, 8.1
Unit 2: 4.1
Unit 3: 4.1

Concepts and principles of assessment

Assessment is a way of finding out if learning has taken place. It enables you, the assessor, to ascertain if your learner has gained the required competence, skills knowledge and understanding needed at a given point towards their programme or qualification. You may be teaching and assessing groups and/or individuals within your organisation, assessing online programmes, or assessing individuals in their work environment. Depending upon the location and subject, you will need to devise suitable ways of assessing your learners to check their progress. It could be that assessment materials have already been produced for you, for example, assignments, or you may have to produce your own. You might assess skills, knowledge and understanding for vocational competence, for example, in a classroom or workshop. Or you might use observations and discussions to assess occupational competence, for example, in a work environment.

Assessment is a regular process; it might not be always be formalised, but you will be observing what your learners are doing, asking them questions, and reviewing their progress whenever you are in contact with them. If you also teach or train, your learners will be demonstrating their knowledge and skills regularly, for example through activities and tasks. You are therefore constantly making judgements about their progress, and how they could improve. You should also be aware of the impact that your comments, marks and grades can have on your learners' confidence. Comments and feedback which specifically focus on the activity or work produced, rather than the individual, will be more helpful and motivating to your learners.

The starting point for devising or using assessments should be the programme syllabus or qualification handbook. This should state how your subject should be assessed, and will give information and guidance in the form of an assessment strategy. The awarding organisations will provide information regarding the assessment strategy for each subject, which can usually be obtained via their website.

Activity

Find out who the awarding organisation is for your particular subject and access their website to review the assessment strategy in the syllabus or qualification handbook. Familiarise yourself with the requirements and find out if you have to produce any assessment materials yourself. Find out what other requirements you will need to follow, for example, your organisation's assessment policy, or any specific regulations relevant to your subject.

The purpose of the strategy is to ensure the subject is assessed in accordance with relevant guidance and regulations, to give a quality service to your learners, and maintain the reputation of your organisation and the qualification. The assessment strategy should state how the subject should be assessed, quality assured and subsequent results recorded. It should also state the experience, professional development and qualifications that assessors should hold. Quality-assurance requirements, for example internal and external verification or moderation, will also be stated. Your organisation should also have an assessment policy which should be followed.

Assessment should not be confused with evaluation, assessment is of the *learner*, evaluation is of the *programme*. Assessment is specific towards learners' achievements and how they can improve. Evaluation is also a quality-assurance monitoring tool. It includes feedback from your learners and others, for example, employers, line managers and verifiers, to help you improve your own practice and the overall learner experience.

Concepts of assessment

A concept is an idea, i.e. what is involved throughout the assessment process and can include:

- accountability;
- achievement;
- assessment strategies;
- benchmarking;
- evaluation;
- initial, formative or summative types;
- internally or externally devised methods (formal and informal);
- progression;
- transparency.

You need to be *accountable* to your learners and your organisation to ensure you are carrying out your role as an assessor correctly. Your learners should know why they are being assessed and what they have to do to meet the assessment criteria. You will also be accountable to the awarding organisation if you assess accredited programmes. You might be accountable to employers if you are assessing their learners in the work environment or bespoke programmes.

You may be required to analyse *achievement* data and compare this to national or organisational targets. The funding your organisation receives might also be related to your learner achievements.

Following the *assessment strategy* for your subject will ensure you are carrying out your role correctly and working towards the required assessor qualifications.

Benchmarking involves comparing what is the accepted standard for a particular subject area against the current position of your own learners' performance. Using benchmarking data can help inform target setting for individuals or groups. If learners don't achieve the benchmark, an evaluation will need to take place and improvements implemented.

Evaluation of the assessment process should always take place to inform current and future practice. All aspects of the assessment cycle should be evaluated on an ongoing basis (see the next section).

Types of assessment include *initial, formative, summative* as well as diagnostic tests which ascertain current knowledge and experience. Some types of diagnostic tests can also identify learners with dyslexia, dyspraxia, dysgraphia, dyscalculia, etc. Initial assessment is carried out prior to or at the beginning of a programme to identify your learner's starting point and level. Formative assessment is ongoing, and summative assessment is at the end.

Internally devised assessments might be produced by you or your organisation such as: assignments, projects or questions which will also be marked by you. *Externally* devised assessments are usually produced by an awarding organisation, for example, an examination. Formal assessments usually count towards achievement of a qualification, whereas informal assessments are used to monitor ongoing progress and development.

Progression should be taken into account when assessing learners, i.e. what they are going to do next. It could be another unit of the current qualification, or a higher level of a different qualification, either at your organisation or elsewhere. Progression opportunities should always be discussed with your learner to ensure they are capable of achieveing their aim.

To assist *transparency*, you need to ensure that everyone who is involved in the assessment process clearly understands what is expected. That includes your own interpretation and understanding of the assessment criteria as well as that of your learners. You may need to liaise with your learner's supervisors, colleagues or mentors, or others in your organisation.

Principles of assessment

Principles are rules and functions which are based upon the concepts, for example, how the assessment process is put into practice.

Key principles of assessment include:

- continuing professional development – maintaining currency of knowledge and competency to ensure assessment practice is up to date;
- equality and diversity – ensuring all assessment activities embrace equality, inclusivity and diversity and represent all aspects of society;
- ethics – ensuring the assessment process is honest and moral, and takes into account confidentiality and integrity;
- fairness – activities should be fit for purpose, and planning, decisions and feedback justifiable;
- health and safety – ensuring these are taken into account throughout the full assessment process, carrying out risk assessments as necessary;
- motivation – encouraging and supporting your learners to reach their maximum potential at an appropriate level;

- quality assurance – an integrated process ensuring assessment decisions meet the qualification standards, and assessors are carrying out their role correctly;

- record keeping – ensuring accurate records are maintained throughout the learning and assessment process, communicating with others, for example, an awarding organisation;

- SMART – ensuring all assessment activities are specific, measurable, achievable, realistic and timebound;

- standardisation – ensuring the assessment requirements are interpreted accurately and that all assessors are making comparable and consistent decisions.

Another important principle is known as VACSR – ensuring all assessed work is:

- **V**alid – the work is relevant to the assessment criteria;

- **A**uthentic – the work has been produced solely by the learner;

- **C**urrent – the work is still relevant at the time of assessment;

- **S**ufficient – the work covers all the assessment criteria;

- **R**eliable – the work is consistent across all learners, over time and at the required level.

Following the concepts and principles of assessment will ensure you are performing your role as an assessor according to all relevant regulations and requirements. All these aspects will all be explored further throughout this book.

Extension Activity

Look at the bulleted lists for the concepts and principles and describe how each will impact upon your role as an assessor. You may need to research some aspects further or speak to relevant staff at your organisation.

The assessment cycle

Depending upon the subject you are assessing and whether it is academic (theory) or vocational (practical), you will usually follow the assessment cycle (see Figure 1.1). The cycle will continue until all aspects of the qualification have been successfully achieved by your learner, or they leave the programme. Records must be maintained throughout to satisfy your organisation, the regulatory authorities and Awarding Organisations.

- Initial assessment – ascertaining if your learner has any previous knowledge or experience of the subject or topic to be assessed. Relevant initial assessment activities will also give you information regarding your learners; for example, any specific assessment requirements they may have, their learning style, or any further training and support they may need.

- Assessment planning – agreeing suitable types and methods of assessment with each learner, setting appropriate target dates, involving others as necessary – for example colleagues or workplace supervisors – and following relevant organisational guidelines.

- Assessment activity – these relate to the methods used, i.e. assessor led, for example observation or questioning; or learner led, for example completing assignments or gathering appropriate evidence of competence. Records of what was assessed should always be maintained.

- Assessment decision and feedback – making a judgement of success or otherwise. Giving constructive feedback and agreeing any further action that may be necessary.

- Review of progress – the assessment plan can be reviewed and updated at any time until your learner completes or decides to leave. Reviewing progress with your learners will give you an opportunity to discuss any other issues that may be relevant to their progress. Reviewing the assessment activities used will give you the opportunity to amend them if necessary.

Figure 1.1 Assessment cycle

The cycle will then begin again with an initial assessment regarding the next subject area or unit of the qualification. Throughout the cycle standardisation of assessment practice between assessors should take place; this will help ensure the consistency and fairness of decisions and that you all interpret the requirements in the same way. Internal verification/moderation will also take place as part of the quality assurance process.

Example

Cameron had planned to give his learners a test to check their progress so far, prior to moving on to the next topic. He had prepared a multiple-choice test containing 30 questions to be completed within one hour. He decided to change the layout of the room from tables in groups to tables in rows. When the learners arrived, they were confused as to what was happening, some became stressed and upset when told they were to take a test. When Cameron marked the tests, most of the learners had not achieved the pass mark. After considering why, he realised he had been so focused on producing the test, he had forgotten to inform the learners about it. He had gone straight into the assessment activity part of the cycle without planning it with the learners first.

Assessment can take place in different environments depending upon what is being assessed and why. Some examples are:

- classroom – activities, tests, role-play, projects, presentations;
- hall – exams;
- library or home – assignments, research;
- outside environment – practical activities;
- workplace – observations and questions;
- workshop – practical tests and simulations.

Wherever you are assessing you will need to ensure both you and your learners are suitably prepared, and that you follow the assessment strategy and relevant guidelines. Assessment should focus on improving learning, while helping your learner achieve their qualification. It should help your learners realise how they are progressing, and what they need to do to improve.

Extension Activity

Find out what documents you need to use to support the assessment process at your organisation. Are they available in hard copy format, or can you access them electronically? Compare them with the ones in Chapter 7 to see if any improvements or changes might be needed. Explain how each document relates to the various functions of the assessment cycle.

Roles and responsibilities of an assessor

Your role and responsibilities will include a lot more than assessing your learners. For example:

- attending meetings, exhibitions, award ceremonies, presentation events;
- carrying out assessments according to the awarding organisation requirements;
- checking the authenticity of any witness testimonies;
- completing and maintaining safe and secure records;

- countersigning other assessors' judgements;

- dealing with any appeals made against your assessment decisions;

- following organisational and regulatory body procedures;

- giving constructive and developmental feedback to your learners;

- identifying and dealing with any barriers to fair assessment;

- implementing internal and external verifier action points;

- liaising with others involved in the assessment process;

- making judgements based on the assessment criteria;

- maintaining occupational competence;

- negotiating and agreeing assessment plans;

- making best use of different assessment types and methods;

- providing statistics to managers;

- reviewing learner progress;

- standardising practice with other assessors;

- supporting learners with special assessment requirements, dealing with sensitive issues in a supportive manner;

- working towards relevant qualifications.

If you are unsure of any aspect of your assessor role or responsibilities, make sure you ask a colleague or your manager. You may be the only assessor for your particular subject within your organisation; therefore it is important that you liaise with your manager or internal quality assurer/moderator to ensure you are interpreting the subject or qualification requirements correctly. If you are a member of a team of assessors, you will need to ensure you all work together to give your learners equal and fair access to assessment opportunities. You will need to attend regular meetings, and work as a team to support the development of your learners.

The assessment process is a systematic procedure which should be followed to give your learner a positive experience, keep them motivated, and help them achieve their aim. During each phase of the assessment cycle, you will perform certain roles, and have responsibilities which should have been defined in your job description. You may be employed purely to assess learners, or you might also teach or train. If you don't have a specific job description for your assessor role from your organisation, the awarding organisation will usually have guidance for you to follow.

If you only assess, you might not consider yourself as a teacher or trainer, but you might find you are guiding, mentoring, coaching or supporting your learners informally in some way.

Example

Joan is assessing the level 2 Award in Floristry. She visits each learner once a month in their place of work to observe their competence, and asks questions to check knowledge. While carrying out an assessment with Ben, she realises he is not quite competent. Joan demonstrates how to perform one of the tasks expected and then Ben has a go. Joan asks Ben to practise this over the next few days, and then she will return the following month to carry out a formal assessment.

In this example, Joan has carried out a coaching session with Ben by demonstrating the task and then encouraging him to do it. If you are demonstrating something in front of a group of learners, always check if they are left- or right-handed as this could change the way they see things. When they look at you, your right hand will be on their left. If you are demonstrating on a one-to-one basis, try to stand or sit next to your learner rather than facing them.

Vocational qualifications are an excellent way for competent staff to demonstrate their skills and knowledge in their work environment, and to gain a qualification. However, if there are aspects of the qualification they are not familiar with, training will need to take place. This might occur with the knowledge and understanding requirements. If you issue a series of questions to test these, all the questions must be answered correctly. Questions should not be marked with grades, for example, A, B or C: they are either right or wrong. If a question is not answered correctly, then the learner will need to redo it. An initial assessment for each unit would greatly help identify what may need to be learnt first, before any assessment takes place. If you are not familiar with how to teach or train, you can take a relevant qualification.

As an assessor, you will need to follow various regulations: for example, the Health and Safety at Work Act (1974). This places a legal responsibility upon you, as well as your organisation and your learners. If you see a potential hazard, you must do something about this before an accident occurs.

Activity

Locate the Health and Safety policy within your organisation, read it to check you understand the contents, and find out who you would go to if you had any problems or queries. If you are assessing in a work environment, make sure you know the details of what you should do and who you should contact if a problem occurs.

You might have to carry out a *risk assessment* to ensure the assessment activity and area are safe for all concerned. This is a requirement under the Management of Health and Safety at Work Regulations (1999), and can normally be achieved by a walk-through of the area, and a discussion with those involved. However, a formal record must be kept in case of any incidents. You probably unconsciously carry out a risk assessment whenever you do anything; for example, when crossing the road, you would automatically check the traffic flow before stepping out. The health and safety of yourself, your colleagues and your learners is of paramount importance. The Health and Safety Executive has produced a useful leaflet which can be accessed at: **www.hse.gov.uk/services/education/information.htm**.

You will need to follow your organisation's policies and procedures, which should include:

● access and fair assessment;

● appeals and complaints;

● copyright and data protection;

● equal opportunities;

● equality and diversity;

● health and safety.

When you commenced your job role, you should have been given information regarding these. If not, make sure you are familiar with them together with other relevant policies and procedures.

Your role as an assessor will also be to inspire and motivate your learners. If you are enthusiastic and passionate about your subject, this will help to stimulate and challenge your learners. Your learners may already be motivated for personal reasons and be enthusiastic and want to perform well. This is known as *intrinsic motivation*. Your learners may be motivated by a need to learn, for example to gain a qualification, promotion or pay rise at work, known as *extrinsic motivation*. If you can recognise the difference between your learners' *wants* and *needs*, you can appreciate why they are motivated and ensure you make their experience meaningful and relevant. Whatever type of motivation your learners have will be transformed, for better or worse, by what happens during their assessment experience. Some learners may lack self-confidence, or have previous experiences of assessment that were not very positive. Many factors can affect your learners' motivation; therefore you need to ensure you treat all your learners as individuals, using their names, and making the assessment experience interesting and meaningful to them. Some learners may need more attention than others. Just because one learner is progressing well doesn't mean you can focus on those that aren't; all your learners need encouragement and feedback. You may not be able to change the environment or the resources you are using, but remaining professional and making the best of what you have will help encourage your learners' development.

Example

Frank has a group of learners working towards a GCSE in Geography. One of his learners, Rea, seems to be losing motivation and is not paying attention during sessions. As Frank knows she enjoys working with computers, he arranges for the class to move to the computer workshop to use the BBC 16+ website, which has activities and tests for learners to complete. These will give immediate scores which will help Frank monitor his learners' progress, and retain the motivation of Rea and the group.

You need to encourage your learners to reach their maximum potential. If you use assessment activities which are too difficult, learners may struggle and become frustrated and anxious. If assessments are too easy, learners may become bored. Knowing your learners and differentiating for their needs will help their motivation.

If you have learners who are quite motivated already, keep this motivation alive with regular challenges, and constructive and positive feedback. A lack of motivation can lead to disruption and apathy. If you are teaching or training as well as assessing, ensure you are reaching the different learning styles of your learners. It might be part of your responsibility to test your learners for their preferred style of learning. A learning styles test could be carried out as part of the initial assessment process. Fleming (1987) categorised learning styles as *visual*, *aural*, *read/write* and *kinaesthetic*, often referred to as VARK.

Activity

Carry out a search via the internet for learning styles, or ask in your organisation which learning styles tests they recommend. Compare different theorists and styles, some tests are more complex than others. Fleming's is available at www.vark-learn.com.

Knowing what style your learners are will help you plan suitable assessment activities. You might not be able to change the *formal* assessments required as part of the programme or qualification, but you might be able to devise *informal* assessments to suit your learners.

Example

Susan had always assessed her learners by assignments and tests. After encouraging them to take a learning styles test, she realised several of her learners are kinaesthetic. She has therefore changed some of her informal assessments to include role play and practical activities.

Using assessment methods which cover all learning styles will ensure you are being inclusive and differentiating for their needs. It also makes the activities more interesting to your learners.

As an assessor, you will have professional boundaries within which to work. You will need to know what these are at your organisation, and not overstep them. Boundaries are about knowing where your role as an assessor stops. You may have a learner who needs more support than others; you would not be helping them if you did their work for them. You would be better guiding them to where they could find things out for themselves, giving them autonomy in the learning and assessment process. You may have some learners who have personal problems and not feel confident at giving them advice. Knowing whom to refer them to would ensure they receive expert information. Always remain professional, don't get personally involved with your learners and don't bring your own problems or attitudes to a situation.

Look at your job description; it might be part of your contract of employment. If you don't have one, look at the information contained in the awarding organisation's syllabus or qualification handbook. Describe the functions you will carry out as an assessor and explain what your responsibilities will be. Find out if your work will be sampled by an internal verifier or moderator and, if so, who this will be and what they will do. Research professional associations you could join which are relevant to assessors.

Communicating with others

You will need to communicate with other people who are involved in the assessment process of your learners. You should remain professional at all times, you are representing your organisation and, although people may not always remember your name, you may be known as 'that person from XYZ organisation'. You therefore need to create a good and lasting impression of yourself and your organisation. You may have to deal with inspectors and auditors from the various stakeholders involved with your programme or qualification. They will need to satisfy themselves that you are capable of assessing the programme or qualification correctly.

People you may need to communicate with, besides your learners, include those internal to your organisation, for example:

- administrators;
- colleagues;
- exam officers;
- internal verifiers/moderators;
- managers;
- mentors;
- other teachers and assessors involved with your learners;
- support staff.

You may also need to liaise with people who are external to your organisation, for example:

- employers;
- external verifiers/moderators;
- funding body staff;
- inspectors;
- parents, guardians, or carers;
- regulatory body staff;
- staff at training events and exhibitions, etc.;

- staff from other organisations and agencies;

- witnesses and others involved in the assessment of your learners.

You might teach a particular subject, but not assess it; for example, your learners may take an exam which is marked by the awarding organisation, or a test which is marked by a colleague. You might have to plan for examinations to take place, in which case you will need to ensure the administration staff are aware of what will take place and when, as invigilators may be needed, and specific rooms timetabled accordingly.

If you are assessing learners in their place of work, it is best to plan ahead to arrange your visits according to location, for example, assessing learners in close proximity to ease the time and cost spent travelling. When assessing in the workplace, notify your learners' employers in advance, in case there is any reason they can't accommodate you on a particular day.

Some of your learners might use a witness testimony as part of their evidence. This will usually come from someone who is an expert at the subject, and knows your learner. They will write a statement of how your learner has met the required outcomes; however, you will need to liaise with them to confirm the authenticity of the statement. All witnesses should sign a declaration, which is usually supplied by the awarding organisation body, and they may require a copy of the witness's certificates and curriculum vitae. If witnesses are involved, they will need to be briefed as to what they are expected to do, and should be familiar with the qualification being assessed.

Where there are different markers or assessors involved with the same qualification, or even the same group of learners, you will need to meet to discuss how you have reached your decisions, and compare the marks given. You might double-mark one another's work to ensure you are all being consistent. Prior to any assessments taking place, you would all need to ensure you have interpreted the assessment requirements and any marking schemes correctly.

If your subject or qualification is quality-assured, your internal and external quality assurer/ moderators will sample your work to ensure your judgements are correct and fair.

Some learners might have a mentor, someone who is supporting and encouraging them while they go through the learning and assessment process. They may also have other teachers, trainers and tutors who are involved with their progress. However, do be aware of any sensitive or confidential issues relating to your learners which they may not wish you to pass on. Conversely, you may need to inform others of any particular learner requirements to ensure consistency of support.

You may act differently depending upon the circumstances. For example, informally with colleagues, but formally with managers and employers. Communication can be verbal, non-verbal or written. Whichever method you use, communication is a means of passing on information from one person to another.

Skills of communicating effectively include the way you speak, listen and express yourself, for example with body language and written information. You need to be confident and organised with what you wish to convey; the way you do this will give an impression of yourself. You may have to attend meetings or video conferences, and wherever you are with other people, they will make assumptions about you based on what they see and hear. You may have to write reports, memos or emails; the way you express yourself when writing is as important as when speaking.

You will not have a second chance to make a first impression, therefore it is important to portray yourself in a professional way, not only with what you say, but in the way you say it, your attitude, body language and dress. A warm and confident smile, positive attitude, self-assurance and the use of eye contact will all help when communicating, particularly if you are meeting someone for the first time.

It could be that you need to write reports of progress for parents or guardians. If you have learners who are attending a programme in conjunction with a school, you may need to liaise with their staff. You may need to communicate with employers or managers/supervisors whose staff you are assessing. If this is the case, make sure you are aware of any protocols involved, and follow your organisation's procedures.

Activity

Find out who you need to communicate with, either internally or externally, regarding the subjects you are assessing. How can you contact them? Make a note of telephone numbers, addresses, websites, emails, etc.

When communicating verbally, your tone, pace and inflections are all important factors in getting your message across. If you speak too quickly or softly, others may not hear everything you say; always try to speak clearly. It is useful to consider what reactions you want to achieve from the information you are communicating, and if others react differently, you will need to amend your methods. You may be communicating via the telephone, therefore unable to see any reactions to your words, which could lead to a misunderstanding. Always ask questions to check that the person you are communicating with has understood what you have said.

Non-verbal communication includes your body language and posture, for example gestures, and the way you stand or sit. Be conscious of your mannerisms, for example folded arms, hands in pockets, or the gestures you make, etc., and use eye contact with the person you are communicating with. The things you don't say are as important as those you do say.

Written communication, for example in the form of feedback for assessed work, or an email, is also an expression of you. The way you convey your words and phrases, and your intention, may not be how it is read or understood by the other person. If you are working with learners via an online programme, you may never see them, but will probably build up a visual image; they may therefore be doing the same of you. Information can be easily misinterpreted; therefore the sender has to be sure the receiver will interpret any communication in the way that it was intended. You need to get your message across effectively; otherwise what you are conveying may not necessarily reflect your own thoughts and may cause a breakdown in communication. Any written text cannot be taken back, so there is less room for errors or mistakes and you need to be clear about the exact meaning you wish to convey. Your writing style, words and syntax need checking for spelling, grammar and punctuation. Don't rely on a computer to check these, as it will not always realise the context in which you are writing. This is particularly the case when writing feedback to learners; if you make a spelling mistake, they will think it is correct as you are the more knowledgeable person.

You might give feedback to your learners via a computer: for example an email or an e-assessment program. If you use this type of medium for communication and/or assessment purposes, try not to get in the habit of abbreviating words or cutting out vowels. It is important to express yourself in a professional way, otherwise misunderstanding and confusion may arise. Just imagine you are talking to the other person, and type your message appropriately.

Example

Aasif has a good professional working relationship with his group. He needs to email his learners to remind them that the room they will be in next week is to be changed due to examinations taking place in their usual room. He keeps his email brief and to the point by stating: 'Hi all, just a quick reminder that we will be in room G3 next week instead of G5, Aasif.' A bad alternative could have been: 'Hey, I told u last week we wld be in a different room cos of exams, so don't forget where u have to go, and dont get lost, A.'

The latter is unprofessional, is rather negative, contains errors, and doesn't convey where the learners should go. This would not give a good impression, and the learners may lose some respect for Aasif.

You may need to liaise with support staff within your organisation, perhaps to arrange help with preparing assessment materials and resources, or by making modifications or adaptations to equipment and materials. Some of your learners may need extra support with literacy or numeracy; if this is arranged make sure you check on their progress. You might also need to get in touch with others who have an involvement with your learners, for example, careers advisers, probation officers or social workers. If this is the case remember aspects of confidentiality, and keep notes of all discussions in case you need to refer to them again.

You might have learners who have excelled in some way, and your organisation or Awarding Organisation may have an award or medal they could be nominated for. Your own organisation or department could hold a celebration event to present certificates to successful learners. This is also a way of obtaining positive publicity for your organisation.

Knowing who you need to deal with, how you should proceed, and what is involved in the assessment process should make your role as an assessor more rewarding and professional.

Extension Activity

Research two theories of communication such as Berne's (1973) Transactional Analysis Theory and Belbin's (1993) Team Role Descriptors. Analyse how these might impact upon your role as an assessor as well as the assessment process with your learners.

Summary

In this chapter you have learnt about:

- concepts and principles of assessment;

- the assessment cycle;

- roles and responsibilities of an assessor;

- communicating with others.

Theory focus

References and further information

Belbin, M. (1993) *Team Roles At Work.* Oxford: Elsevier Science & Technology.

Berne, E. (1973) *Games People Play: The Psychology of Human Relationships.* London: Penguin Books Ltd.

Health and Safety Executive (1999) *Management of Health and Safety at Work Regulations – Approved Code of Practice and Guidance* (2nd edn). London: HSE Books.

Tummons, J. (2011) *Assessing Learning in the Lifelong Learning Sector* (3rd edn). Exeter: Learning Matters.

Wallace, S. (2007) *Teaching, Tutoring and Training in the Lifelong Learning Sector* (4th edn). Exeter: Learning Matters.

Wilson, L. (2008) *Practical Teaching – a Guide to PTLLS and CTLLS.* London: Engage Learning.

Websites

Chartered Institute for Educational Assessors – **www.ciea.org.uk**

Fleming's Learning Styles – **www.vark-learn.com**

Health and Safety Executive – **www.hse.gov.uk**

Office Safety & Risk Assessments – **www.officesafety.co.uk**

2 PLANNING FOR ASSESSMENT

Introduction

> In this chapter you will learn about:
>
> - assessment planning.
>
> - types of assessment;
>
> - supporting learners;
>
> - equality and diversity within assessment.

There are activities and examples to help you reflect on the above which will assist your understanding of the assessment planning process.

At the end of each section is an extension activity to stretch and challenge your learning further.

This chapter contributes towards the following: scope (S), knowledge (K) and practice (P) aspects of the professional standards (A–F domains) for teachers, tutors and trainers in the Lifelong Learning Sector.

AS1, AS2, AS3, AS5, AS6;
AK1.1, AK2.1, AK3.1, AK4.1, AK5.1, AK5.2, AK6.1, AK6.2, AK7.1, AK7.3;
AP1.1, AP2.1, AP2.2, AP3.1, AP4.1, AP5.1, AP5.2, AP6.1, AP6.2, AP7.1, AP7.3;
BS1, BS2, BS3, BS4, BS5;
BK1.1, BK1.2, BK1.3, BK2.2, BK3.4, BK3.5, BK4.1, BK5.2;
BP1.1, BP1.2, BP1.3, BP2.1, BP2.2, BP2.3, BP2.5, BP3.5, BP4.1, BP5.1, BP5.2;
CS2, CS3, CK3.2, CK3.3, CK3.5;
CP2.1, CP3.2, CP3.3, CP3.5, CP4.2;
DS1, DS2, DS3;
DK1.1, DK2.1, DK2.2;
DP1.1, DP1.3, DP2.1, DP2.2;
ES1, ES2, ES3, ES5;
EK1.1, EK1.2, EK2.1, EK2.2, EK2.3, EK3.1, EK3.2, EK5.1, EK5.2, EK5.3;
EP1.2, EP2.1, EP2.2, EP2.4, EP3.1, EP3.2;
FS1, FS2, FS4;
FK1.1, FK1.2, FK2.1, FK4.1, FK4.2;
FP1.1, FP1.2, FP2.1, FP3.1, FP4.1, FP4.2.

This chapter contributes towards the following Learning and Development Assessor Units:

Unit 1 – 3.1, 3.2, 3.3, 3.4, 3.5, 4.1, 4.2, 4.4, 4.4, 5.2, 8.3
Unit 2 – 1.1, 1.2, 1.3, 1.4, 4.2
Unit 3 – 1.1, 1.2, 1.3, 2.2, 4.2

Assessment planning

Assessment gives a measure of learning at a given point in time. Relevant skills, knowledge, understanding and/or attitudes can be measured towards a subject or qualification.

Subjects that don't lead to a formal certificate are known as non-accredited; if a subject is accredited, it is through an awarding organisation and a certificate will be issued upon successful completion by the learner. They will monitor the delivery and assessment of the qualification to ensure all their guidelines are being followed.

Before you commence any assessment planning with your learners you need to be fully conversant with the programme or qualification you are going to assess, along with any relevant policies, requirements and regulations for your particular subject. You then need to ascertain whether your learners can be assessed straight away or if they need any further training or practice beforehand. It could be that you teach your learners as well as assess them, in which case you will have an idea of when they will be ready for assessment. You will also have agreed an individual learning plan (ILP) with them which outlines what they will be working towards. However, if you don't teach your learners but just assess them in their working environment it will be more difficult to know when they will be ready. You will need to agree an assessment plan with each of your learners to outline what will be assessed, when and how.

Careful assessment planning and prior knowledge of your learners' previous achievements are the key to ensuring everyone involved understands what will take place and when.

Prior to assessing your learners' progress towards their chosen subject, you need to carry out an initial assessment or training needs analysis to ascertain their skills and knowledge so far. These will include specific activities relating to the subject or qualification your learners will be taking. The results of these will help you plan what needs to be learnt and assessed, and can also trigger the process known as recognising prior learning (RPL).

Example

Sharron has completed an initial assessment which was designed to evaluate her knowledge and skills towards the level 2 Diploma in Travel and Tourism. Sharron had started the qualification at another organisation prior to moving to the area. Her assessor was able to see that she had already been assessed for three units fairly recently. Sharron was therefore accredited with these units once her assessor had confirmed all the requirements had been met. She therefore did not need to be reassessed.

You might also carry out a diagnostic assessment to see if your learners require any support with aspects such as literacy and numeracy.

Initial assessment will help to:

- agree an appropriate individual learning plan or assessment plan, with suitable targets;
- allow for differentiation and individual requirements to be met;
- ensure learners are taking the right programme at the right level;
- identify an appropriate starting point for each learner;
- identify any information which needs to be shared with colleagues;
- identify any specific additional support needs;
- identify learners' previous experience and achievements, using it as a foundation for further learning and assessment;
- identify learning styles;
- identify specific requirements, for example, the Functional Skills of maths, English and information and communication technology (ICT);
- inspire and motivate learners;
- involve learners, giving them confidence to agree targets.

Activity

Find out what initial and diagnostic assessments are used at your organisation. Will it be your responsibility to administer these, or is there a specialist person to do this? How will you use the results to help plan what your learners will do and when?

There are lots of initial assessment materials available online. If you get the opportunity, carry out a search for *initial assessment* or *diagnostic assessment*.

The starting point for planning your assessment will be the syllabus. However, the subject or qualification you are assessing might not have a syllabus, or it could be called something else, such as:

- course outline;
- course specification;
- programme guidelines;
- qualification handbook;
- set of standards.

Most syllabi can be obtained directly from the awarding organisation via their website. However, if you are assessing a non-accredited programme, you may be working from a syllabus produced by your organisation, or you may even have to write your own. The language used within the syllabus to denote what will need to be taught and assessed will usually be written as one of:

- ability outcomes;

- aims and objectives;

- assessment criteria;

- evidence requirements;

- learning outcomes;

- performance criteria;

- standards;

- statements of competence.

Assessment should be a two-way process between you and your learners; you need to plan what you are going to do, and they need to know what is expected of them.

The way you plan to assess your learners will depend upon the:

- assessment method and type;

- assessment strategy;

- awarding organisation requirements;

- conditions for assessment;

- dates, times and duration;

- learners and level;

- level;

- location and environment;

- organisational budget;

- requirements for making decisions and giving feedback;

- resources and materials;

- special requirements or learner needs;

- staff availablity and expertise;

- subject or qualification, i.e. workplace competence, vocational or academic;

- type of evidence required.

If you are assessing a subject with all the information and materials provided by the awarding organisation, the process of planning should be quite straightforward.

However, you will still need to carry out some form of assessment planning, and inform your learners when assessment will take place and how. If you prepare a scheme of work, you will need to ensure time is planned for the relevant assessments, along with time for feedback. If your learners are working towards a formal qualification, you will need to ensure they have been registered with the appropriate awarding organisation. It might not be your responsibility to carry out this task, but you should communicate the details of your learners to relevant staff. If a record of attendance or an in-house certificate will be issued to your learners, this information should be communicated to the person who will issue them. You will should inform your learners when they can expect to receive any feedback or formal recognition of their achievements. You should discuss what they can do if they disagree with the assessment planning process, such as whom they could go to if they couldn't resolve an issue. Completing an assessment plan and review record will formalise the process; an example is available in Chapter 7.

You might assess on an individual basis within your organisation, or at your learner's place of work. Or you might assess group work such as role-play or discussions in a classroom. If it is the latter, you would need to assess each individual's contribution towards the assessment requirements. Otherwise you would be passing the whole group, when some may not have contributed much at all. If you are related to, or know personally, the learners you will assess, you should notify your organisation of any conflict of interest. They may also need to notify the relevant awarding organisation, in case you are not allowed to assess a learner if they are a direct member of your family, or your spouse's family.

Assessment planning should be specific, measurable, achievable, realistic and time bound (SMART).

- Specific – the activity relates only to the qualification and assessment criteria being assessed and is clearly stated.

- Measurable – the activity can be measured against the qualification and assessment criteria, allowing any gaps to be identified.

- Achievable – the activity can be achieved at the right level.

- Realistic – the activity is relevant and will give consistent results.

- Time bound – target dates and times are agreed.

Planning SMART assessment activities will ensure all the criteria will be met by your learners, providing they have acquired the necessary skills and knowledge beforehand.

Activity

Have a look at the syllabus or qualification handbook for the subject you will assess. What are the assessment requirements or criteria? Do they begin with words such as explain, describe or demonstrate? These will give you an idea of how you can plan to assess your learners. Are there any formal assessment materials provided such as assignments or case studies? Can you create some informal assessment materials to assess ongoing progress before administering the formal assessments? If so, consider what you could create, for example, devising a role-play.

Assessment planning should provide opportunities for both you and your learners to obtain and use information about progress towards the required outcomes. It should also be flexible in order to respond to any emerging ideas and skills, for example the use of new technology. The way you plan should include strategies to ensure that your learners understand what they are working towards, and the criteria that will be assessed. You should also plan how and when you will give your learners feedback. It could be verbally immediately after the assessment, the next time you see them, or by email or another written means.

Wherever possible, you should try to assess holistically. This enables your learner to demonstrate several aspects of a qualification at the same time. For example, they might be taking several units, the content of which might be similar, or they might be taking a performance unit which incorporates aspects of a knowledge unit. Rather than assessing each separate unit, you could assess all the similar criteria at the same time. Holistic assessment should make evidence collection and demonstration of competence much more efficient.

Example

Rafael is due to assess Sheila for the L3 Certificate in Assessing Vocational Achievement which consists of the following three units.

1. *Understanding the principles and practice of assessment;*

2. *Assess occupational competence in the work environment;*

3. *Assess vocational skills, knowledge and understanding.*

Units 2 and 3 have almost identical assessment criteria for learning outcomes 3 and 4. Rafael is therefore able to plan to assess these all at the same time, providing Sheila can provide the required evidence.

Holistic assessment is beneficial to all concerned when assessing occupational competence, particularly in a work environment. You may be able to observe naturally occurring situations in addition to what had originally been planned. Learners might be able to demonstrate several learning outcomes from different units at the same time depending upon their job role, for example, aspects of health and safety. Rather than planning to assess individual units on different occasions, you could discuss your learner's job role with them to identify which learning outcomes from all of the units could be demonstrated at the same time. While the assessment might take longer, it would reduce the number of visits and therefore the inconvenience to all involved. Your learner would need to be ready to demonstrate their competence, therefore don't plan to assess unless they are confident. Never arrange to assess your learner if they are not ready, as this could demoralise them and waste time. You could also involve witnesses, other people the learner is in contact with who could give a statement or testimony as to their competence.

It could be that you carry out a holistic assessment and find your learner is competent at most but not all of the criteria you planned to assess. If this is the case, you can still sign off what they have achieved and then update the assessment plan to assess the remaining criteria on another occasion. Alternatively, you might be able to ask questions or involve witnesses to give evidence regarding the gaps, if this is acceptable.

Portfolios of evidence

Some qualifications require learners to produce a portfolio of evidence. This is a file containing evidence which proves their achievements and can be manual or electronic. This is an ideal opportunity for learners to cross-reference the evidence they provide across several units, learning outcomes and assessment criteria. There's no need for them to reproduce any evidence, they can just give the piece of evidence a number and quote this number against the relevant assessment criteria it meets. If this is the case, your learner should have a copy of the qualification's requirements to help them see what is involved. You can both refer to these when planning the types of evidence which will be provided, and how and when you will assess the evidence. With any portfolio, it's about the quality of the evidence, not the quantity. When you are assessing evidence, you don't want to be spending a lot of time searching for something and your internal quality assurer or moderator won't want to either. Some qualifications might require you as the assessor to cross-reference the evidence rather than the learner. If this is the case, you will need to plan what is required and by when, encouraging your learner to self-assess their evidence towards the relevant criteria before giving it to you.

It could be that your learner has achieved some units of the qualification elsewhere and might just need to provide their certificate as evidence of prior achievement. If the achieved units are listed on the Qualifications and Credit Framework (QCF), they will automatically be recognised providing your learner has a unique learner number (ULN). This number will track all units achieved which are on the framework. Learners will be able to view an online record of their achievements and can give access to others who might wish to check what has been achieved previously. This system will be useful to learners and reduce fraud. For example, if a learner has an interview for a job but has lost their paper-based qualifications, they will be able to access their online record to prove their achievements.

Assessment planning should be short term and long term, to allow for formative and summative assessment to take place. Including your learners in the planning process will help identify what they have learnt, how and when they will be assessed, and allow for communication to take place to clarify any points or concerns. Encouraging an open dialogue will help learner motivation, and build up a climate of trust. Enabling your learners to assess themselves against the relevant criteria will help them identify their own strengths and limitations, providing opportunities for further development if necessary.

When planning to assess, you should have a rationale; consider: *who, what, when, where, why* and *how* (WWWWWH). This information should always be agreed with your learners beforehand. If you are assessing on an individual basis, the assessment planning process should be formalised, and an assessment plan completed and agreed. The plan should reflect what will be assessed, by whom, where and when the assessment will take place, why it is taking place, and how it will take place. When the assessment takes place, the plan will be reviewed to reflect what has been achieved and when using the WWWWH approach, will ensure you are setting SMART targets with your learners.

Example

<table>
<tr><td colspan="7">

Assessment plan and review

Learner: Irene Jones   Assessor: Jenny Smith

Qualification and level: Level 1 Certificate in Hospitality   Unique learner number: 1234567891

Date commenced: 6 September   Expected completion date: 17 December
</td></tr>
<tr>
<td>Date</td>
<td>Aspect of qualification

(unit/learning outcome or assessment criteria)</td>
<td>Date achieved</td>
<td>Assessment details

Planning – methods of assessment, activities and SMART targets

Review – revisions to plan, achievements and issues discussed</td>
<td>Target/ review date</td>
<td colspan="2">Agreed by
(assessor and learner to sign)</td>
</tr>
<tr>
<td>10 Sept</td>
<td>**Unit 101**

Maintain a safe, hygienic and secure working environment</td>
<td></td>
<td>Planning – an observation will take place on 6 October at the County Leisure Centre to formatively assess competence in the workplace.

Oral questions will be asked and a professional discussion will take place based on the knowledge requirements.

A witness testimony will be obtained from Irene's supervisor.

Irene has a copy of the unit requirements and we have discussed the following learning outcomes of unit 101 today:

1. Be able to maintain personal health and hygiene.
2. Know how to maintain personal health and hygiene.
3. Be able to help maintain a hygienic, safe and secure workplace.
4. Know how to maintain a hygienic, safe and secure workplace.</td>
<td>6 Oct</td>
<td colspan="2">*J Smith*

I Jones</td>
</tr>
</table>

The assessment plan is like a written contract between you and your learner, towards the achievement of their qualification. It can be reviewed, amended and updated at any time.

Some assessments will not require a formal assessment plan, but you must always be SMART when setting assessment activities, and discuss the process with your learners.

Gabriel is due to assess her group's interviewing skills. She has informed them she will carry out an observation using a checklist during next week's session. The checklist covers the assessment criteria and clearly states what each learner must demonstrate, within a five minute interview. Gabriel has given a copy to her learners and has therefore been SMART with her assessment planning. She will give immediate feedback to her learners afterwards.

When planning assessments, you will need to take into account equality of opportunity, inclusivity and differentiation within the assessment process.

Consider the WWWWWH of assessment for your particular subject. Create an assessment plan using the pro-forma in Chapter 7 or use one from your organisation. Ensure your plan meets the SMART requirements. Will you need to involve anyone else when creating the plan (besides the learner), such as another teacher, assessor, witness or workplace supervisor? What impact will this have upon the assessment process?

Types of assessment

Different subjects will require different types of assessment, which can be carried out formally or informally depending upon the requirements. Formal assessments are usually planned and carried out according to the assessment criteria, whereas informal assessments can occur at any time, to check ongoing progress. You may be familiar with some types such as initial (at the beginning), formative (ongoing) and summative (at the end). You may not be as familiar with other terms such as ipsative, norm, or criterion referencing.

Assessment *types* are different assessment methods. A method is how the assessment type will be used.

Formal assessment methods can include:

- assignments;
- essays;
- exams;
- observations;
- oral and written questions;
- multiple-choice questions;
- recognising prior learning (RPL);
- tests.

Informal assessment methods can include:

- discussions;

- gapped handouts (cloze sentence/missing words);

- journals/diaries;

- peer feedback;

- puzzles and quizzes;

- role play.

All these methods and more are explored further in Chapter 3. All assessment methods and types should be suitable to the level of your learners. A level 1 learner might struggle to maintain a journal of their progress and a level 2 learner may not be mature enough to accept peer feedback. A level 3 learner may feel a puzzle is too easy, and so on. Some learners may respond better to informal formative assessment rather than formal summative assessment. You need to consider the assessment requirements for your subject, and how you can best implement these, without changing the assessment criteria.

Example

Maria sees her group of learners once a week for an Art and Design programme. Each week, she commences the session by asking some questions regarding the topics covered in the previous week. This is informal formative assessment to ensure her learners have understood the topics taught. At the end of term, she will issue a summative assignment, which will formally test their skills and knowledge.

Questions are a really useful type of formative assessment, to ensure your learners are acquiring the necessary knowledge before moving on to a new topic. They can also be useful as a type of summative assessment at the end of a programme.

When planning which assessment type to use, you need to ensure it will be *valid* and *reliable*, and that you are being *fair* and *ethical* with all your decisions.

- Valid – the assessment type is appropriate to the subject/qualification being assessed.

- Reliable – if the assessment is carried out again with similar learners, similar results will be achieved.

- Fair – the assessment type is appropriate to all your learners at the required level, is inclusive, i.e. available to all, and differentiates for any particular needs.

- Ethical – the assessment takes into account confidentiality, integrity, safety, security and learner welfare.

These aspects must always be considered carefully to ensure you are only assessing what is necessary and relevant, at a level to suit your learners, and that there is no chance of favouritism occurring with assessment decisions.

The style of qualification you assess will also determine the assessment type used, for example an academic programme could be summatively assessed by an exam, whereas a vocational programme could be formatively assessed by observation and questioning.

Decide upon the types of assessment you will use for your subject. How will you ensure they are valid, reliable, fair and ethical? Are they appropriate for the levels of your learners? Look at the table on pages 35–37 for ideas.

You might have all the details of assessment types and methods provided for you; if not, you will need to carefully select these to suit your subject, the situation and your learners. You might decide to assess your learners on a formative basis throughout their time with you, with a summative test at the end. This would enable you to see how they are progressing, and whether they will be ready or not prior to taking the final summative test. You might be provided with assignments for your learners to complete at set times during the programme. To be sure your learners are ready you could use activities, quizzes and tasks for your learners to carry out prior to the assignments. This would make the assessment process more interesting, and highlight any areas which need further development. If you are assessing a programme whereby the activities are provided for you, for example tests or exams, there is often the tendency to teach purely what is required to achieve a pass. Learners may therefore not gain valuable additional skills and knowledge. Teaching to pass tests does not maximise your learners' ability and potential.

Bloom (1956) believed that education should focus on the mastery of subjects and the promotion of higher forms of thinking, rather than an approach which simply transfers facts. Bloom's Taxonomy (1956) model attempts to classify all learning into three overlapping domains. These are:

1. *cognitive domain* (intellectual capability, i.e. knowledge or thinking);

2. *affective domain* (feelings, emotions and behaviour, i.e. attitudes or beliefs);

3. *psychomotor domain* (manual and physical skills, i.e. skills or actions).

The three domains are summarised as knowledge, attitudes and skills, or *think*, *feel*, *do*. Your learners should benefit from the development of knowledge and intellect (cognitive domain); attitudes and beliefs (affective domain); and the ability to put physical skills into effect (psychomotor domain). You would therefore assess your learners at the right level for their learning, at the appropriate time. Each domain contains objectives at different levels, such as, list, describe, explain, and analyse.

Example

Pierre has a group of Level 1 learners working towards a Certificate in Welding Skills. He carries out formative assessment of his learners using objectives such as list and state (to test knowledge), adopt and familiarise (to test attitudes), and attempt and use (to test skills). When he is sure his learners have mastered the topics, he will give them a summative test which will assess the required knowledge, attitudes and skills needed to achieve the certificate.

If Pierre used objectives such as *explain*, *justify* and *facilitate*, these would be too high a level for his learners. If his learners progress to level 2, Pierre would then use higher-level objectives. A comprehensive list of objectives at different levels can be found in the companion book by Gravells and Simpson (2010), *Planning and Enabling Learning in the Lifelong Learning Sector*.

Minimising risks

When planning to assess your learners you need to be aware of potential risks, not only those regarding the health, safety and welfare of all concerned, but the types of risks that may be involved in your own area of responsibility for your particular subject.

You need to minimise risks such as putting unnecessary stress upon learners, over-assessing or being unfair and expecting too much too soon. Some learners might not be ready to be observed for a practical skill, or feel so pressured by target dates for a theory task that they resort to colluding or plagiarising work from others or the internet.

If learners are under pressure, or have any issues or concerns that have not been addressed, they may decide to leave the programme. Being aware of any risks and taking opportunities to discuss any issues your learner might have should help alleviate any concerns.

There are also risks on your part as an assessor, for example, pressure to pass learners quickly due to funding implications or favouritism and bias towards some learners over others. It could be that if you have close friends or relatives whom you need to assess, you might not be allowed to, or your decisions would need to be countersigned by someone impartial.

If there are no clear guidelines or assessment criteria, you might find yourself being subjective rather than objective. That is, you make your own decision without any guidance and therefore base it on your opinion rather than fact.

Activity

Ask a colleague, friend or family member to make a paper plane, and tell them you will assess them while they are doing this. Once they have made it, ask them to fly it and give them a grade of pass, refer or fail.

How did they do and what helped you make your decision? Was it a pass because they made the plane and it flew for a few seconds? Was it a referral because they made the plane but it didn't fly, or was it a fail because they didn't know how to make a paper plane, you just assumed they could? Without any criteria to assess against, you will be making a subjective decision, which could be wrong. Following assessment criteria will ensure your assessment is valid and reliable, and you are being fair and ethical.

If you have a group of learners whom you are testing, for example, using written questions to check their knowledge which may be graded, i.e. A–E, you will need to produce expected responses to ensure you are being fair when marking. If you don't you might find yourself subconsciously giving a higher mark to the best learners in your group. You should always remain objective when assessing, not have any favourite learners, and follow the marking criteria correctly. Otherwise, you may find your learners may appeal against your decision.

If you want to compare the achievements of your group against one another, you could use *norm-referencing*. This would proportion your marks accordingly, as there will always be those in your group who will achieve a high mark, those who will achieve a low mark, leaving the rest in the middle. You would allocate your marks according to a quota, for example, the top 20 per cent would achieve an A, the next 20 per cent a B, and so on. Norm-referencing uses the achievement of a group to set the standards for specific grades, or for how many learners will pass or fail. This type of assessment is useful to maintain consistency of results over time; whether the test questions are easy or hard, there will always be those achieving a high grade or a lower grade, whatever their marks.

Example

Petra has a group of 25 learners who have just taken a test consisting of 20 questions – she wants to allocate grades A–E to her group. She has worked out the top 20 per cent will achieve an A, the second 20 per cent a B and so on. When she marks the tests, she is surprised to see the lowest mark was 16 out of 20, meaning a grade E. Even though the learner had done well in the test, they were still given a low grade in comparison to the rest of the group.

A fairer method of marking would have been to set a pass mark, for example, 15 out of 20. Learners achieving 14 or below could retake a different test at a later date.

Criterion-referencing enables learners to achieve based upon their own merit, as their achievements are not compared with one another. All learners therefore have equality of opportunity. If grades are allocated, for example a distinction, credit or pass, there will be specific criteria which must have been met for each. Either these criteria will be supplied by the awarding organisation, or you may need to produce them yourself.

Example

Pass – described the activity.

Credit – described and analysed the activity.

Distinction – described, analysed and critically reflected upon the activity.

The following table summarises various types of assessment. The ones you use will be based on whether you assess vocational skills, knowledge and understanding or occupational competence.

Academic	Assessment of theory or knowledge.
Aptitude	A diagnostic test to assess your learner's ability for a particular job or vocation.
Assessor led	Assessment is planned and carried out by the assessor, for example an observation.
Benchmarking	A way of evaluating learner performance against an accepted standard. Once a standard is set, it can be used as a basis for the expectation of achievements within other groups/learners.
Competence based	Criteria that learners need to perform in the work environment.
Criterion referencing	Assessing what your learner *must achieve* to meet a certain standard.
Diagnostic	A specific assessment relating to a particular topic or subject and level, which builds on initial assessment. Sometimes called a *skills test*. The results determine what needs to be learnt or assessed in order to progress further. Some types of diagnostic assessments can also identify learners with dyslexia, dyspraxia, dysgraphia, dyscalculia, etc.
Direct	Evidence provided by your learner towards their qualification, for example products from their work environment.
Evidence	Assessment is based upon items your learner provides to prove their competence.
External	Assessments set and marked externally by the relevant awarding organisation.
Formal	Assessment which involves the recognition and recording of achievement.
Formative	Ongoing, interim or continuous assessment. Can be used to assess skills, knowledge and/or understanding in a progressive way, to build on topics learnt and plan future learning and assessments. Often referred to as assessment for learning, allowing further learning to take place prior to more assessments.
Holistic	Assessing several aspects of a qualification at the same time.
Independent	An aspect of the qualification is assessed by someone who has not been involved with your learner for any other part of their training or assessment.
Indirect	Evidence provided by others regarding your learner's progress, for example a witness testimony from their supervisor.
Informal	Assessment which is in addition to formal assessment, for example, questioning during a review of progress with your learner, or an observation during a group activity.

Initial	Assessment at the beginning of a programme or unit, relating to the subject being learnt and assessed, to identify your learner's starting point and level. Initial assessment can also include learning styles tests, and literacy, numeracy and ICT skills scan. The latter can be used as a basis to help and support learners.
Integrated	Information acquired in a learning context is put into practice and assessed in their work environment.
Internal	Assessments carried out within an organisation, either internally set and marked, or externally set by the relevant awarding organisation and internally marked.
Ipsative	A process of self-assessment. Learners match their own achievements against a set of standards, or keep a reflective journal of their learning so far. This is useful for learners to see their own progress and development; however, they do need to work autonomously and be honest about their achievements.
Learner led	Learners produce evidence, or let their assessor know when they are ready to be assessed.
Norm-referencing	Comparing the results of learner achievements with one another, for example setting a pass mark to enable a certain percentage of a group to achieve or not.
Objective	An assessment decision which is based around the criteria being assessed, not a personal opinion or decision.
Proficiency	An assessment to test ability, for example, riding a bike.
Process	The assessment of routine skills or techniques is assessed, for example, to ensure your learner is following a set procedure. Or Additional learning will take place besides that stated to achieve the assessment criteria.
Product	The outcome is assessed, not the process. For example a painting or a working model. Or Teaching only the minimum amount required to pass an assessment.
Profiling	A way of recording learner achievements for each individual aspect of an assessment. Checklists can be a useful way to evidence these. More than one assessor can be involved in the process.
Qualitative	Assessment is based upon individual responses to open questions given to your learners. Clear criteria must be stated for the assessor to make a decision, as questions can be vague or misinterpreted.
Quantitative	Assessment is based upon yes/no or true/false responses, agree/disagree statements, or multiple-choice tests, giving a clear right or wrong answer. Totals can be added to give results, for example 8 out of 10. Learners could pass purely by guessing the correct answers.
Screening	An informal process to assess if your learner has a language, literacy, numeracy or ICT skills need.
Subjective	A personal decision by the assessor, where the assessment criteria may not be clearly stated. This can be unfair to your learner.

Summative	Assessment at the end of a programme or unit, for example, an exam. If your learner does not pass, they will usually have the opportunity to retake. Often known as assessment of learning, as it shows what has been achieved from the learning process.
Triangulation	Using more than one assessment method, for example, observation, oral questioning and a test. This helps ensure the reliability and authenticity of your learner's work and makes the assessment process more interesting.
Vocational	Job-related practical assessment, usually in your learner's work environment.

Extension Activity

Refer to the **types of assessment table** *and choose six types that you might use with your learners. Summarise the types of risks that might be involved when using them and explain how you could minimise risks when planning assessments with your learners.*

Supporting learners

All learners are entitled to a fair assessment and should be given the best opportunity to demonstrate their ability. Whichever type and methods of assessment you choose, you need to support and treat each learner as an individual as their needs may be different. Initial assessments should have identified most needs; however, always ask your learners if there is anything you can do to support their learning.

Example

If you have a dyslexic learner it may be appropriate to ask questions rather than give a written test, or have someone to scribe their responses. For a partially sighted learner you could give papers in a larger font or use a magnified reading lamp. For a deaf learner, you could give a written test instead of an oral test. For a learner with Asperger's syndrome, you could use written questions rather than oral questions. For some learners who might struggle with spelling and grammar, the use of a computer could help. An adapted keyboard or a pen grip could help a learner with arthritis.

Some learners may have barriers to assessment, for example access to a particular room, transport or health problems. Some learners may require additional support with literacy and numeracy. You may also have to challenge your own values and beliefs if you don't agree with those of your learners to ensure you remain professional at all times. Some learners may have a support assistant who will be present during the assessment. They will be there to help your learner in case they have any difficulties. Make sure you address your learner, not their assistant, to ensure you are including them fully in the process. If you have a learner with a speech impediment, give them time to finish speaking before continuing.

Examples of meeting learner needs include the following.

- A disability – learners could be assessed in a more comfortable environment or location where appropriate access and support systems are available.

- A hearing impairment – an induction loop could be used where all or part of an assessment is presented orally. Instructions and questions could be conveyed using sign language.

- A visual impairment – using large print or Braille, using specialist computer software if available, asking questions verbally and making an audio recording of your learner's responses.

- Cultural or religious requirements – such as a prayer room or refreshments to suit various diets.

- Dyslexia – allowing additional time if necessary and/or the use of a word processor to type responses. Presenting written questions in a more simplified format, for example, bullet points and using pastel-coloured paper and printing in a different font. Or asking questions verbally and making an audio or visual recording of your learner's responses.

- English as a second or other language – using an interpreter or sign language; if possible try to arrange assessments in your learner's first or bilingual language, for example, Welsh. Many awarding organisations can translate assessment materials if requested:

- Learner support – generic support relating to the learning and assessment experience, for example, advice, counselling, crèche, transport, etc. You may need to liaise with others.

- Learning support – specific support relating to the achievement of the qualification, the functional skills of English, maths and ICT, help with study and research skills, support with academic writing and referencing, using Braille or larger print.

- Learning styles – adapting the assessment activities to suit the styles of the learners.

- Levels of learning – using different activities, for example, quizzes for lower-level learners, written questions for higher levels.

- Varying assessment types and methods such as using new and emerging technology to assess distantly.

- Varying work patterns – trying to be flexible and arranging the assessment at a time and place to suit both learner and assessor.

- Welfare – learners could be given extra time to allow for emotional or personal issues, or dates for assessment could be rearranged to fit around doctor or hospital appointments. Learners might need to take medication privately, which could interrupt an assessment, for example, an insulin injection.

If you need to adapt any assessment activities for an accredited qualification, you will need to check with the awarding organisation first. You may need to liaise with others in your organisation regarding any specific needs that you are not able to help with, for example, using an interpreter or lip reader.

Activity

Look at the assessment activities you are going to use with your learners: what support might you give to your learners based upon their needs, and how would you go about arranging this? What aspects of your learner's welfare might you be responsible for? Consider emotional aspects as well as physical.

You might be familiar with what you can and cannot do, but you may need to find out with whom you should liaise regarding your learners' needs and their welfare. Always check with your organisation and awarding organisation to ensure you are following their regulations. You cannot change a set examination date and time without approval, and you may need consent in writing for other changes or amendments to assessments.

If you have a learner requiring support for any reason, there is a difference between *learning support* and *learner support*. Learning support relates to the subject, or help with language, literacy, numeracy or information communication technology (ICT) skills. Learner support relates to any help your learner might need with personal issues, and/or general advice and guidance regarding their welfare.

Always ask your learners how you can help them, but try to avoid making them feel different or uncomfortable. If you are unsure of what you can do to help your learners, ask your supervisor or manager at your organisation. Don't just assume you are on your own to carry out any amendment to provision; there will be specialist staff to help.

Never assume everything is fine just because your learners don't complain. Always include your learners in the assessment planning process in case there is something you don't know that you need to act upon.

When planning assessment activities, you need to know when your learners are ready. There's no point assessing them if they haven't learnt everything they need to know, as you will be setting them up to fail. If your learner has been absent for any reason, make sure you update them regarding what they have missed. Carrying out a formative assessment well before a summative assessment can help both you and your learner see how ready they are.

The timing of your assessments can also make a difference: if you plan to assess on a Friday before a holiday period, your learners may not be as attentive; equally so first thing on a Monday morning. This is difficult of course if you see your learners only on these particular days. If you are planning a schedule of assessments throughout the year, you will need to consider any public or cultural holidays. There is no point planning to assess every third Monday if the majority of these fall on public holidays. You might also need to assess your learner in their place of work. If they work shifts or during the weekend you would need to visit when they are working, as it isn't fair to ask them to change their work patterns just to suit you. If for any reason an assessment is cancelled, make sure a revised date is scheduled as soon as possible, inform all concerned and update the assessment plan.

Extension Activity

Think about your learners and the environment in which you will be assessing them. Do you need to ask your learners if any adaptations or changes are required? Will the timing of the assessments impact on your learners in any way, for example during an evening session when they may not have had time to eat? Find out what you are allowed to amend in accordance with regulations. Check what documentation and guidance your Awarding Organisation provides to support learner needs.

Assessment planning is a crucial part of the teaching and learning process. If this is not carried out correctly and comprehensively, problems may occur which could disadvantage your learners and prevent them from being successful.

Equality and diversity within assessment

All learners should have equality of opportunity within assessment, providing they are taking a programme they are capable of achieving. There's no point setting learners up to fail, just because you needed a certain number of learners for your programme to go ahead, perhaps due to targets or funding. When designing assessment activities, you need to ensure you meet the needs of all your learners, and reflect the diverse nature of your group. Never let your own attitudes, values and beliefs interfere with the assessment process. You need to cover all the required assessment criteria, but you could design activities which will challenge more able learners and/or promote the motivation of learners who are not progressing so well. You need to differentiate your activities to ensure you are meeting the needs of all your learners, while adhering to any organisational and awarding organisation requirements. Your organisation will have an Equal Opportunities or Equality and Diversity policy which you should become familiar with. You might have a learner who achieves tasks quickly; having more in-depth activities available and ready to use would be beneficial to them. If you have learners who are not achieving the required assessment tasks, design an activity that you know they will achieve, to raise their motivation and encourage them to progress further. However, don't oversimplify activities which will leave learners thinking they were too easy. You could always give your learners a choice of, for instance, a straightforward, a challenging or a very challenging activity. The choice may depend upon the confidence level of your learners, and you will have to devise such activities beforehand if they are not provided for you. If you have different levels of learners within the same group, this can work quite well as they will usually want to attempt something they know they can attain. However, it can also have the opposite effect in that learners feel they are more capable than they actually are.

Example

Elaine is assessing her group of learners for the Award in Preparing to Teach in the Lifelong Learning Sector. She has a mixed group of level 3 and level 4 learners. All of the learners opt to take the level 4 assessment tasks. However, once Elaine marks their responses, she realises most of them only meet the criteria for level 3. When she informs them of this, they do not take the feedback well.

In this example, all the learners felt they were capable of a higher level of achievement, and were therefore demoralised when told they were not to the required standard. If an initial assessment had been carried out beforehand, the learners would be aware of their abilities and which level to work towards.

Assessment activities should always reflect the diverse nature of the group, for example, culture, language and ethnicity. They should not be biased according to the person producing them; otherwise aspects such as terminology or jargon might not be those of the learners, but those of the producer, placing the learner at a disadvantage. You also need to be careful not to discriminate against your learner in any way.

Example

Jo has a group of 20 learners taking a programme in Photography. The learners are aged between 16 and 70, with a variety of religions and cultural backgrounds. They are mainly male and have various past experiences of the subject. Two of Jo's learners use a wheelchair, one is dyslexic and two have diabetes. For their next assignment, Jo has asked them to take a photograph of an object, one that represents something special to the learners. This assignment has been planned not to discriminate against anyone, and is therefore inclusive to all.

The Equality Act (2010) replaced all previous anti-discrimination legislation and consolidated it into one act (England, Scotland and Wales). It provides rights for people not to be directly discriminated against or harassed because they have an association with a disabled person. People must not be directly discriminated against or harassed because they are wrongly perceived as disabled.

Previous terminology such as: age, disability, gender, race, religion, belief, sexual orientation, marriage, civil partnership, pregnancy and maternity are now known as *protected characteristics*.

There are seven different types of discrimination.

1. Associative discrimination: direct discrimination against someone because they are associated with another person with a protected characteristic.

2. Direct discrimination: discrimination because of a protected characteristic.

3. Indirect discrimination: when a rule or policy which applies to everyone can disadvantage a person with a protected characteristic.

4. Discrimination by perception: direct discrimination against someone because others think they have a protected characteristic.

5. Harassment: behaviour deemed offensive by the recipient.

6. Harassment by a third party: the harassment of staff or others by people not directly employed by an organisation, such as an external consultant or visitor.

7. Victimisation: discrimination against someone because they made or supported a complaint under equality legislation.

Activity

How do you think the seven different types of discrimination will impact upon your role as an assessor? Will they affect your learners in any way?

Amendments could include using words like *person* instead of *man*, or using pictures in a handout to reflect different races and cultures.

When planning assessments, you need to consider any particular requirements of your learners, to ensure they can all participate. Initial assessment would ensure your learners are able to take the subject; however, you may need to adapt resources, equipment or the environment to support them. If anything is adapted, make sure both you and your learners are familiar with them prior to carrying out the assessment activity. You cannot change the assessment criteria issued by the awarding organisation, but you could change the way you implement the assessment process. If you need to make any changes, you must consult the relevant awarding organisation to discuss these. Most will have an *Access to Assessment* document which will inform you what you can and cannot do.

You can help your learners by organising your environment to enable ease of access around any obstacles (including other learners' belongings), along corridors, and around internal and external doors. When assessing, ensure you face your learners when speaking, to assist anyone hard of hearing, produce clearly printed handouts in a font, size and colour to suit any particular learner requirements. Always ask your learners if there is anything you can do to help make the assessment experience a positive one.

Your organisation should have support mechanisms to meet any special assessment requirements or individual needs of learners.

Examples include learners with issues such as the following.

- Dyspraxia – allow additional time and space if necessary for learners who have poor motor co-ordination.

- Dysgraphia – allow learners the use of a computer or other suitable media for learners who have difficulty with handwriting.

- Dyscalculia – allow additional time if necessary and use calculators or other equipment for learners who have difficulty with calculations or maths.

- Dyslexia – allow additional time or resources if necessary for learners who have difficulty processing language. Present written questions in a more simplified format, for example bullet points. Ask questions verbally and make an audio or visual recording of your learner's responses; allow the use of a laptop for typing responses rather than expecting handwritten responses.

- A disability – learners could be assessed in a more comfortable environment where appropriate access and support systems are available. Learners could be given extra time to complete the assessment tasks, or to take medication privately. Dates could be rearranged to fit around doctor or hospital appointments.

- A hearing impairment – an induction loop could be used where all or part of an assessment is presented orally. Instructions and questions could be conveyed using sign language.

- A visual impairment – use large print or Braille, use specialist computer software if available, ask questions verbally and make an audio recording of your learner's responses.

- Varying work patterns – try to schedule the assessment at a time and place to suit.

- English as a second or other language – if allowed, try to arrange assessments in your learner's first language, for example, in Welsh. Many awarding organisations can translate assessment materials if requested. Bilingual assessments should also be offered.

All learners should have equality of opportunity and appropriate support to enable them to access assessment. Your organisation needs to ensure they follow the requirements of any relevant legislation such as the Disability Discrimination Act (DDA) 1995. The DDA was passed to protect disabled people from discrimination. According to the DDA, *a person has a disability if he or she has a physical or mental impairment, which has a substantial and long-term adverse effect on his/her ability to carry out normal day to day activities.*

It could be that you do not need to make any special arrangements just yet, but knowing what to do, and who to go to, will make things easier for you when the time does occur.

In September 2002 the DDA was extended to include education, which broadened the rights of disabled people. Under Part 4 of the Act, colleges and local authorities (LAs) have legal responsibilities:

- not to treat disabled learners less favourably for reasons related to their disability;

- to provide reasonable adjustments for disabled learners.

You need to anticipate the likely needs of disabled learners and not merely respond to individual needs as they arise. The Act uses a wide definition of disabled person to include: *people with physical or sensory impairments, dyslexia, medical conditions, mental health difficulties and learning difficulties.* Educational organisations have a duty to take reasonable steps to encourage learners to disclose a disability. This could be part of your learner application, interview process and/or initial assessment procedure and encouragement should be ongoing throughout the programme. If your learner does disclose a disability or additional need to anyone, including you as their assessor, then the whole organisation is *deemed to know.* It is therefore important that any issues are communicated to all other staff concerned, and acted upon.

From 2005, organisations have had to make *reasonable adjustments* to the physical features of their premises to overcome physical barriers to access. This could include the provision of ramps to classrooms, and access to disabled toilets. Desks are now available with adjustable legs which can be raised for wheelchair access, and specialist equipment is available to adapt resources. You may need further training to familiarise yourself with any particular assessment requirements to meet your learners' needs. You also need to know the names of staff at your organisation who are responsible for equality and diversity, and learner support.

Safeguarding

Safeguarding is a term used to refer to the duties and responsibilities that those providing a health, social or education service have to carry out/perform to protect individuals and vulnerable people from harm. Following the publication of the Safeguarding Vulnerable Groups Act in 2006, a vetting and barring scheme was established in autumn 2008. This Act created an Independent Barring Board to take all discretionary decisions on whether individuals should be barred from working with children and/or vulnerable adults. As an assessor, you will be bound by this Act.

Every Child Matters (ECM)

The Children Act (2004) provided the legal underpinning for the Every Child Matters: Change for Children programme. The terms *learner*, *adult* or *citizen* are often used when teaching post-16 learners instead of *child*. Well-being is the term used in the Act to define the five Every Child Matters outcomes which should be taken into account when you are in contact with your learners. These are:

- be healthy;
- stay safe;
- enjoy and achieve;
- make a positive contribution;
- achieve economic well-being.

Ways to embed the outcomes of Every Child Matters include:

- being healthy – access to drinking water and healthy food; opportunities to keep active;
- staying safe – maintaining a safe environment; health and safety training;
- enjoying and achieving – opportunities for all learners to enjoy and achieve a relevant qualification; recognising transferable skills;
- making a positive contribution – group activities, role-play and teamwork; citizenship, voluntary work and work experience;
- achieving economic well-being – business and enterprise activities; becoming independent and autonomous, gaining employment.

Further details regarding equality and diversity can be found in the companion book by Gravells and Simpson (2009) *Equality and Diversity in the Lifelong Learning Sector*.

Extension Activity

Find out what policies and procedures your organisation has to promote equality and diversity, and identify those which you think are working and those which are not. What can you do to make improvements? What do you think the challenges would be for your organisation and yourself?

Summary

In this chapter you have learnt about:

- assessment planning;

- types of assessment;

- supporting learners;

- equality and diversity within assessment.

Theory focus
References and further information

Bloom, B.S. (1956) *Taxonomy of Educational Objectives, the Classification of Educational Goals – Handbook I: Cognitive Domain.* New York: McKay.

Department for Education and Skills (DfES) (2006) *Safeguarding Children and Safer Recruitment in Education.* London: DfES.

Gravells, A. and Simpson, S. (2010) *Planning and Enabling Learning in the Lifelong Learning Sector* (2nd edn). Exeter: Learning Matters.

Websites

Assessment guidance booklets – **www.sflip.org.uk/assessment/ assessmentguidance.aspx**

Disability and the Equality Act – **http://tinyurl.com/2vzd5j**

Equality and Human Rights Commission – **www.equalities.gov.uk**

Every Child Matters – **www.dcsf.gov.uk/everychildmatters**

Initial Assessment Tools – **www.toolslibrary.co.uk**

Literacy and Numeracy online tests – **www.move-on.org.uk**

Quality Improvement Agency – **http://excellence.qia.org.uk**

Introduction

> In this chapter you will learn about:
>
> ● methods of assessment;
>
> ● the role of ICT within assessment;
>
> ● questioning;
>
> ● making assessment decisions.

There are activities and examples to help you reflect on the above which will assist your understanding of the various methods of assessment, and how to make assessment decisions.

At the end of each section is an extension activity to stretch and challenge your learning further.

This chapter contributes towards the following: scope (S), knowledge (K) and practice (P) aspects of the professional standards (A–F domains) for teachers, tutors and trainers in the Lifelong Learning Sector.

AS1, AS2, AS3, AS5, AS6;
AK2.1, AK3.1, AK5.1, AK5.2, AK6.1, AK6.2;
AP1.1, AP2.1, AP2.2, AP3.1, AP5.1, AP5.2, AP6.1, AP6.2;
BS1, BS3, BS4, BS5;
BK1.1, BK1.3, BK2.2, BK3.2, BK3.5, BK4.1, BK5.1, BK5.2;
BP1.1, BP1.3, BP2.1, BP2.2, BP2.3, BP2.4, BP2.5, BP3.1, BP3.5, BP4.1, BP5.1, BP5.2;
CK3.2, CK3.3, CK3.5, CK4.1, CK4.2;
CP1.1, CP3.5, CP4.2;
DS1;
DP1.1;
ES1, ES2, ES3;
EK1.2, EK1.3, EK2.1, EK2.2, EK2.3, EK2.4, EK3.1, EK3.2, EK4.1, EK5.1, EK5.2, EK5.3;
EP1.1, EP1.2, EP1.3, EP2.1, EP2.2, EP2.3, EP3.1, AP3.2, EP5.5.

This chapter contributes towards the following Learning and Development Assessor Units:

Unit 1 – 2.1, 4.3, 5.1, 8.2
Unit 2 – 2.1, 2.2
Unit 3 – 2.1, 2.3, 2.4

Methods of assessment

There are several different ways of assessing to ensure learning has taken place; for example, observation, questioning, tests and exams. If these activities are not provided by the awarding organisation you will need to devise your own. The methods you choose will depend upon whether you are assessing performance, i.e. skills, or knowledge, i.e. understanding. You would take into account your learners' needs, their level, and the subject requirements before planning a suitable method. Assessment can only take place once learning has occurred.

Activity

Think about the learners you have at present, or those whom you will be assessing in the future. How do you know that learning has taken place and that they will be ready to be assessed?

You might be able to answer this by saying, 'I'll ask questions', or 'I'll see them working'. That's fine, if you know what questions to ask and how your learners should respond, or what you expect to see your learners do. To effectively plan how you will assess your learners, you need to use a method which is valid and reliable. If you set a test which doesn't accurately reflect the assessment criteria, it will be invalid. If you devise a set of questions, and use them with different groups of learners, they may discuss these among themselves, therefore rendering the questions unreliable.

Assessment can take place at any point in your learners' progress. Initial assessment will give you an appropriate starting point for your learners, giving you information about their skills and knowledge to date. Formative assessment helps you see how your learners are progressing, before moving on to other topics. It also helps you adapt your teaching to cover any additional work which might be necessary. Summative assessment will give a final decision as to your learners' achievements. If you are assessing your learners during a teaching session, remember to allow plenty of time for this when preparing your scheme of work and session plans.

The results obtained from any assessment activity should be used to adapt and improve teaching and learning. Assessment should reinforce learning as well as measuring what has been learnt.

Assessment can be separated into the needs of the learner, the assessor, the organisation and the awarding organisation.

Learner – to:

- clarify what is expected of them;
- enable discussions with assessors;
- evaluate their own progress;
- have something to show for their achievements, for example a certificate;
- know how well they are doing;
- know they are achieving the correct standard or level;
- know what they have to do next;
- learn from mistakes.

Assessor – to:

- adapt teaching, learning and assessment activities;
- ascertain progress so far;
- certificate learning;
- decide what's next;
- develop learners' self-assessment skills;
- diagnose any learner needs or particular learning requirements;
- empower learners to take control of their learning;
- follow the requirements of the awarding organisation;
- grade learners;
- improve motivation and self-esteem;
- prepare learners for further assessments;
- prove they can assess effectively;
- recognise efforts and achievements;
- share judgements and practice with others;
- structure stages of progress.

Organisation – to:

- achieve funding;
- analyse enrolment, retention and achievement rates;
- ensure consistency between assessor practice;
- give references for learners if requested;
- identify gaps in learning;
- justify delivery of programmes;

- maintain records;

- promote a learner-centred approach;

- satisfy awarding organisation requirements;

- standardise decisions between assessors.

Awarding organisation – to:

- accredit achievements;

- ensure compliance with regulations and qualification requirements;

- set standards.

Assessment should never be just for the sake of assessing. There should always be a reason for any assessment activity you carry out, the main one being to find out if learning has taken place.

You might have found it easy to design the activity, but when you used it with your learners, it wasn't as effective as you would have liked. You need to take into account:

- any specific requirements within the syllabus;

- equality and diversity;

- the criteria you are assessing;

- the environment, facilities and resources;

- the need to be specific, measurable, achievable, realistic and time bound (SMART);

- the abilities, levels and needs of your learners;

- the reliability and validity of the type and method used;

- *who, what, when, where, why* and *how* (WWWWWH) you will assess.

Never be afraid to try something different, particularly with formative assessments that you can design yourself. You could use puzzles, quizzes or crosswords as a fun and active way of informally assessing learner progress. Try searching the internet for free software to help you create these.

You might have thought about using different types and methods to give a varied approach to address all learning styles. You might use a blended approach to incorporate the use of technology with other methods. If you have different levels of learners within the same group, you could use the same activities, but with different assessment criteria, for example *list, describe, explain,* or *analyse.*

Extension Activity

Consider how you will assess your learners for your specialist subject.
What methods will you use and why?

The role of ICT within assessment

Technology is constantly evolving and new resources are frequently becoming available. It's crucial to keep up to date with new developments and try to incorporate these within the assessment process. It's not only about you using technology to help assess your learners, but about your learners using it to complete their assessment activities. Encouraging your learners to use technology will help increase their skills in this area. Technology can be combined with traditional methods of assessments; for example, learners can complete a written assignment by word-processing their response and submitting it by email or uploading it to a secure website. You can then give informal feedback via email and follow this up with written and verbal feedback when you next see your learner. Combining methods also promotes differentiation and inclusivity; for example, learners could access assessment materials via a virtual learning environment (VLE) outside the normal learning environment to support learning within the classroom.

New and emerging technologies include using:

- blogs, chat rooms and online discussion forums to help learners communicate with each other;
- cameras and mobile phones for taking pictures;
- computer facilities for learners to word-process their assignments and save documents and pictures;
- digital media for visual/audio recording and playback;
- electronic portfolios for learners to store their work;
- email for electronic submission of assessments, communication and informal feedback on progress;
- interactive whiteboards for learners to use and display their work;
- internet access for research to support assignments;
- mobile phones for taking pictures, video and audio clips and communicating;
- networked systems to allow access to programs and documents from any computer linked to the system;
- online and on-demand tests which can give instant results, for example, diagnostic and multiple-choice tests;
- online discussion forums which allow asynchronous (taking place at different times) and synchronous (taking place at the same time) discussions;
- presentation software and equipment for learners to give presentations;
- scanners for copying and transferring documents to a computer;
- web cameras or video conferencing if you can't be in the same place as your learners and you need to observe a task;
- VLEs to upload supporting materials and assessment activities.

There will be advantages and limitations when using technology. Advantages are that they are:

- auditable and reliable;
- accessible and inclusive;
- addresses sustainability, i.e. no need for paper copies;
- efficient use of time and cost-effective;
- immediate results can be obtained from online tests;
- learners can access resources and materials at a time and place to suit;
- tests can be on demand.

Limitations might be that:

- they can lead to plagiarism of text via the internet;
- they cannot be used during power cuts;
- finance is required to purchase new technology and computers;
- they might create barriers if learners cannot access or use technology;
- not enough resources are available for all learners to use at the same time;
- some learners might be afraid of using new technology;
- they are time-consuming to initially set up.

If you are planning on working towards your teaching status of Associate or Full Qualified Teacher Learning and Skills (ATLS/QTLS), you will need to evidence the minimum core of ICT to at least level 2.

In March 2005 the Department for Education, Children's Services and Skills published the e-Strategy *Harnessing Technology: Transforming learning and children's Services*. This strategy describes the use of digital and interactive technologies to achieve a more personalised approach within all areas of education and can be accessed at: **www.dcsf. gov.uk/publications/e-strategy/**.

Extension Activity

Design an assessment activity to use with your learners, preferably incorporating ICT. This could be a formative activity to test progress to date. Use it with your learners and then evaluate how effective it was. What changes would you make and why?

The following table lists the assessment methods and activities you could use, with a brief description, and the strengths and limitations of each. When using any activities, you need to ensure they are inclusive, and differentiate for individual learning styles and needs, learner difficulties and/or disabilities. Always follow health and safety guidelines, and carry out any relevant risk assessments where applicable. Make sure your learners are aware why they are being assessed, and don't overcomplicate your activities.

Method	Description	Strengths	Limitations
Assignments	Several activities or tasks, practical or theoretical, to assess various aspects of a qualification over a period of time	Can challenge a learner's potential Consolidates learning Several aspects of a qualification can be assessed Some assignments are set by the awarding organisation who will give clear marking criteria	Ensure all aspects of the syllabus have been taught beforehand Can be time-consuming to prepare and assess Must be individually assessed and written feedback given Assessor might be biased when marking
Blended assessments	Using more than one method of assessment, usually including technology	Several methods of assessment can be combined, enabling all learning styles to be reached	Not all learners may have access to the technology
Buzz groups	Short topics to be discussed in small groups	Allows learner interaction and focuses ideas Checks understanding Doesn't require formal feedback	Learners may digress Specific points could be lost Checking individual learning has taken place may be difficult
Case studies/ scenarios	Can be a hypothetical situation, a description of an actual event or an incomplete event, enabling learners to explore the situation	Can make topics more realistic, enhancing motivation and interest Can be carried out individually or in a group situation Builds on current knowledge and experience	If carried out as a group activity, roles should be defined and individual contributions assessed Time should be allowed for a de-brief Must have clear outcomes Can be time-consuming to prepare and assess
Checklists	A list of criteria which must be met to confirm competence or achievement	Can form part of an ongoing record of achievement or profile Assessment can take place when your learner is ready Ensures all criteria are met and a record maintained	Learners may lose their copy and not remember what they have achieved
Discussions/ debates	Learners talk about a relevant topic which contributes to the assessment criteria	All learners can participate Allows freedom of viewpoints, questions and discussions	Easy to digress Assessor needs to keep the group focused and set a time limit Some learners may not get involved, others may take over – assessor needs to manage the contributions of individuals Can be time-consuming Learners may need to research a topic in advance Can lead to arguments

Method	Description	Strengths	Limitations
e-assessments/ online assessments	*Electronic assessment* – assessment using information and communication technology (ICT) *Synchronous* – assessor and learner are simultaneously present, communicating in real time *Asynchronous* – assessor and learner are interacting at different times	Teaching, learning and assessment can take place in a virtual learning environment (VLE) Assessment can take place at a time to suit learners Participation is widened Results can be instantly generated Ensures reliability Less paperwork for the assessor Improves ICT skills Can be blended with other assessment methods Groups, blogs, forums and chat rooms can be set up to improve communication	Learners need access to a computer and need to be computer literate Self-discipline is needed, along with clear targets Authenticity of learner's work may need validating Technical support may be required Reliable internet connection needed
Essays	A formal piece of written text, produced by your learner, for a specific topic	Useful for academic subjects Can check your learner's language and literacy skills at specific levels	Not suitable for lower-level learners Marking can be time-consuming Plagiarism can be an issue Doesn't usually have a right or wrong answer therefore difficult to grade Learners need good writing skills
Examinations	A formal test which should be carried out in certain conditions	Can be *open book*, or *open notes*, enabling learners to have books and notes with them Some learners like the challenge of a formal examination and cope well	Invigilation required Security arrangements to be in place prior to, and afterwards for papers Learners may have been taught purely to pass expected questions by using past papers, therefore they may forget everything afterwards Some learners may be anxious
Group work	Enables learners to carry out a specific activity, for example, problem solving Can be practical or theoretical	Allows interaction between learners Encourages participation and variety Rotating group members enables all learners to work with each other	Careful management by the assessor is required regarding time limits, progress, and ensuring all group members are clear about the requirements Could be personality problems with team members or large groups One person may dominate Difficult to assess individual contributions Time is needed for a thorough de-brief and feedback

Method	Description	Strengths	Limitations
Holistic	Enables learners to demonstrate several aspects of a qualification at the same time.	Holistic assessment of a performance unit could incorporate aspects of a knowledge unit Similar criteria from different units can be assessed at the same time Makes evidence collection and demonstration of competence much more efficient	Could confuse the learner if aspects were assessed which were not planned for
Homework	Activities carried out between sessions, for example, answering questions, to check knowledge	Learners can complete at a time and place that suits them Maintains interest between sessions Encourages learners to stretch themselves further Consolidates learning so far	Clear time limits must be set Learners might not do it, or get someone else to do it for them Must be marked/assessed and individual feedback given
Icebreakers/team building exercises	A fun and light-hearted way of introducing learners and topics	A good way of learners getting to know each other, and for the assessor to observe skills and attitudes Can revitalise a flagging session	Not all learners may want to take part Some learners may see these as insignificant – careful explanations are needed to link the experience to the topic
Interviews	A one-to-one discussion, usually before your learner commences a programme, or part-way through to discuss progress	Enables the assessor to see how much a learner knows Enables the assessor to get to know each learner, and discuss any issues	Not all learners may react well when interviewed Needs careful planning, and consistency of questions between learners
Learner statements	Learners write how they have met the assessment criteria	Enables learners to take ownership of their achievements	Learners might misinterpret the assessment criteria and/or write too much or too little Another assessment method should be used in addition to confirm competence
Learning journal/diary	Learners keep a record of their progress, their reflections and thoughts, and reference these to the assessment criteria	Helps assess language and literacy skills Useful for higher level programmes	Should be specific to the learning taking place and be analytical rather than descriptive Contents need to remain confidential Can be time-consuming and/or difficult to read
Observations	Watching learners perform a skill	Enables skills to be seen in action Learners can make a mistake (if it is safe) enabling them to realise what they have done wrong Can assess several aspects of a qualification at the same time (holistic assessment)	Timing must be arranged to suit each learner Communication needs to take place with others (if at a learner's workplace) No permanent record unless visually recorded Questions must be asked to confirm understanding Assessor might not be objective with decision

Method	Description	Strengths	Limitations
Peer assessments	Learners giving feedback to their peers after an activity	Promotes learner and peer interaction and involvement Learners may accept comments from peers better than those from the assessor Enables learners to assess each other Activities can often correct misunderstandings and consolidate learning without intervention by the assessor	Everyone needs to understand the assessment criteria and requirements Needs to be carefully managed to ensure no personality conflicts or unjustified comments Assessor needs to confirm progress and achievements as it might be different Some peers may be anxious about giving feedback Should be supported with other assessment methods Needs careful management and training in how to give feedback
Portfolios of evidence	A formal record of evidence (manual or electronic) produced by learners, towards a qualification	Ideal for learners who don't like formal exams Can be compiled over a period of time Learner centred, promotes autonomy Evidence can be left in its natural location and viewed by the assessor	Authenticity and currency to be checked Computer access required to assess electronic portfolios Tendency for learners to produce a large quantity of evidence All evidence must be cross-referenced Can be time-consuming to assess Confidentiality of documents within the portfolio must be maintained
Practical activities/ tasks	Assesses a learner's skills in action	Actively involves learners Can meet all learning styles if carefully set	Some learners may not respond well to practical activities Can be time-consuming to create
Presentations	Learners deliver a topic, often using audio-visual aids	Can be individual or in a group Can assess skills, knowledge and attitudes	If a group presentation, individual contributions must be assessed Some learners may be nervous or anxious Practice sessions are useful, but time-consuming
Products	Evidence produced by your learner to prove competence, for example, paintings, models, video, audio, photos	Assessor can see the final outcome Learners feel a sense of achievement, for example, by displaying their work in an exhibition	Authenticity needs to be checked if the work in progress has not been seen

Method	Description	Strengths	Limitations
Professional discussions	A conversation between the assessor and learner based around the assessment criteria	Ideal way to assess aspects which are more difficult to observe Useful to support observations to check knowledge Learners can describe how they carry out various activities	A record must be kept of the discussion, for example, audio/digital/visual along with notes Needs careful planning as it's a discussion not a question and answer session Learners need time to prepare Assessor needs to be experienced at questioning and listening skills Assessor needs to be experienced at using open and probing questions, and listening carefully to the responses
Projects	A longer-term activity enabling learners to provide evidence which meets the assessment criteria	Can be interesting and motivating Can be individual or group led Can meet all learning styles Encourages research skills Learners could choose their own topics and devise tasks	Clear outcomes must be set, along with a time limit, must be relevant, realistic and achievable Progress should be checked regularly If a group is carrying out the project, ensure each individual's input is assessed Assessor might be biased when marking Thorough feedback should be given
Puzzles, quizzes, word search, crosswords, etc.	A fun way of assessing learning in an informal way	Fun activities to test knowledge, skills and/or attitudes Useful backup activity if learners finish an activity earlier than planned Useful way to assess progress of lower level learners Good for assessing retention of facts	Can seem trivial to mature learners Does not assess your learner's level of understanding or ability to apply their knowledge to situations Can be time-consuming to create and assess
Questions	A key technique for assessing understanding and stimulating thinking Questions can be closed, hypothetical, leading, open, probing, multiple choice, etc.	Can be multiple-choice, short answer or long essay style Can challenge and promote a learner's potential A question bank can be devised which could be used again and again for all learners Can test critical arguments or thinking and reasoning skills Oral questions suit some learners more than others, e.g. a dyslexic learner might prefer to talk through their responses	Closed questions only give a yes or no response which doesn't demonstrate knowledge Questions must be written carefully, i.e. be unambiguous, and can be time-consuming to prepare If the same questions are used with other learners, they could share their answers Written responses might be the work of others, i.e. copied or plagiarised Expected responses or grading criteria need to be produced beforehand to ensure consistency and validity of marking May need to re-phrase some questions if learners are struggling with an answer

Method	Description	Strengths	Limitations
Recognition of prior learning (RPL)	Assessing what has previously taken place to find a suitable starting point for further assessments	Ideal for learners who have achieved aspects of the programme prior to commencement No need for learners to duplicate work, or be reassessed Values previous achievements	Checking the authenticity and currency of the evidence provided is crucial Can be time-consuming for both your learner to prove, and the assessor to assess
Reports, research and dissertations	Learners produce a document to inform, recommend and/or make suggestions based on the assessment criteria	Useful for higher level learners Encourages the use of research techniques	Learners need research and academic writing skills Time-consuming to mark Plagiarism and authenticity can be an issue
Role-plays	Learners act out a hypothetical situation	Enables you to observe learners' behaviour Encourages participation Can lead to debates Links theory to practice	Can be time-consuming Clear roles must be defined Not all learners may want, or be able to participate Some learners may get too dramatic Individual contributions must be assessed Time needed for a thorough de-brief
Self-assessment	Learners decide how they have met the assessment criteria, or are progressing at a given time	Promotes learner involvement and personal autonomy Encourages learners to check their own work before handing in Encourages reflection Learners need to be specific about what they have achieved and what they need to do to complete any gaps	Learners may feel they are doing better than they actually are Assessor needs to discuss progress and achievements with each learner to confirm their decisions Learners need to be specific about what they have achieved and what they need to do to complete any gaps Difficult to be objective when making a decision
Skills tests	Designed to find out the level of skill or previous experience/knowledge for a particular subject or vocation	Could be online or computer based to enable a quick assessment, for example, literacy Results can be used as starting point for learning or progression	Learners might be apprehensive of formal tests Feedback might not be immediate
Simulation	Imitation or acting out of an event or situation	Useful when it is not possible to carry out a task for real, for example, to assess whether learners can successfully evacuate a building in a fire. You don't need to set fire to the building to observe this process	Only enables an assessment of a hypothetical situation, learners may act very differently in a real situation Not usually accepted as NVQ evidence

Method	Description	Strengths	Limitations
Tests	A formal assessment situation	Cost-effective method as the same test can be used with large numbers of learners Some test responses can be scanned into a computer for marking and analysis Other tests can be taken at a computer or online and give immediate results	Needs to be carried out in supervised conditions or via a secure website Time limits usually required Can be stressful to learners Does not take into account any formative progress Feedback might not be immediate Learners in other groups might find out the content of the tests from others Identity of learners needs confirming If set by an awarding organisation, ensure all aspects of the syllabus have been taught beforehand
Tutorials	A one-to-one, or group discussion between the assessor and learner, with an agreed purpose, for example, assessing progress so far	A good way of informally assessing all learner's progress and/or giving feedback An opportunity for learners to discuss issues or for informal tuition to take place	Needs to be in a comfortable, safe and quiet environment as confidential issues may be discussed Time may overrun Records should be maintained and action points followed up
Video/audio	Recorded evidence of actual achievements	Direct proof of what was achieved by your learner Can be reviewed by the assessor, internal verifier/moderator after the event	Can prove expensive to purchase equipment and tapes/discs Can be time-consuming to set up Technical support may be required Storage facilities are required

Method	Description	Strengths	Limitations
Walk and talk	A spoken and visual way of assessing a learner's competence	Enables a learner to *walk and talk* through their product evidence within their work environment Gives an audit trail of the evidence relating to the assessment criteria Saves time producing a full portfolio of evidence, the walk and talk can be recorded as evidence of the discussion Useful where sensitive and confidential information is dealt with	A time-consuming way of assessing the criteria Difficult for verifiers to sample the evidence
Witness testimonies	A statement from a person who is familiar with your learner	The witness can confirm competence or achievements, providing they are familiar with the assessment criteria, for example, a workplace supervisor	The assessor must confirm the suitability of the witness and check the authenticity of any statements Learners might write the statement and the witness might sign it not understanding the content
Worksheets and gapped handouts (known as cloze sentence or missing words)	Interactive handouts to check knowledge (can also be electronic) Blank spaces can be used for learners to fill in the missing words	Informal assessment activity which can be done individually, in pairs or groups Useful for lower-level learners Can be created at different degrees of difficulty to address differentiation	Mature learners may consider them inappropriate Too many worksheets can be boring, learners might not be challenged enough

Questioning

Questions can be oral, i.e. verbally or written, for example open questions requiring a full answer or closed questions requiring a yes or no answer. If you are asking questions verbally to a group of learners, ensure you include all learners. Don't just let the keen learners answer first as this gives the ones who don't know the answers the chance to stay quiet. Ask a question, pause for a second and then state the name of a learner who can answer. This way, all learners are thinking about the answer as soon as you have posed the question, and are ready to speak if their name is asked. This is sometimes referred to as *pose, pause, pounce* (ppp). To ensure you include everyone throughout your session, you could have a list of their names handy and tick each one off after you have asked them a question. This is fine if you don't have a large group. If you do, make sure you ask different learners each time you are in contact with them. When asking questions, only use one question in a sentence, as more than one may confuse your learners. Try not to ask *Does anyone have any questions?*, as often only those that are keen or confident will ask, and this doesn't tell you what your learners have learnt. Try not to use questions such as *Does that make sense?* or *Do you understand?*, as your learners will often say 'yes' as they feel that's what you expect to hear.

Try to use open questions which require an answer to demonstrate knowledge and understanding. For example: *How many days are there in September?* This ensures your learner has to think about their answer. Using a closed question such as *Are there 30 days in September?* would only give a yes/no answer which doesn't show you if your learner has the required knowledge. Open questions usually begin with *who, what, when, where, why* and *how*.

If you are having a conversation with your learner, you can ask *probing* questions to ascertain more information. These can begin with: *Why was that?* You can *prompt* your learner to say more by asking *What about...?* You can clarify what your learner is saying by asking *Can you go over that again?* You can lead your learner by saying *So what you are saying is...* or you can ask a hypothetical question such as *What would you do if...?*

If you have to produce written questions for your learners, think how you will do this, i.e. short questions, essay-style questions with word counts, open, closed or multiple choice. If you are giving grades, e.g. A, B, C, or pass/merit/distinction, you need clear grading criteria to follow to make sure your decisions are objective, otherwise your learners may challenge your decisions.

Multiple-choice questions should have a clear question and three or four possible answers. The question is known as the *stem*, the answer is called the *key* and the wrong answers are called *distracters*. Answers should always be similar in length and complexity. Answers should not be confusing, and there should only be one definite key.

Example

Formative assessment is always:

(a) before the programme commences;

(b) at the beginning of the programme;

(c) ongoing throughout the programme;

(d) when the programme ends.

You will see that all the answers contain a similar amount and type of words. None of the answers contains a clue from the question. A, B and D are the distracters and C is the correct answer (the key).

If you are using the same questions for different learners at different times, be careful as they may pass the answers to each other. You may need to rephrase some questions if your learners are struggling with an answer as poor answers are often the result of poor questions. For essay and short-answer tests you should create sample answers to have something to compare to. Be careful with the use of jargon – just because you understand it doesn't mean your learners will.

You need to be aware of plagiarism, particularly now that so much information is available via the internet. Learners should take responsibility for referencing any sources of all work submitted, and may be required to sign an authenticity statement. If you suspect plagiarism, you could type a few of their words into an internet search engine or specialist program and see what appears. You would then have to challenge your learner as to whether it was intentional or not, and follow your organisation's plagiarism procedure.

Extension Activity

Design a questioning activity to carry out with your learners. This could be some oral questions that you will ask to an individual learner, for example, to check knowledge of a practical task being demonstrated in their work environment. Or it could be a multiple-choice test, short-answer or essay-style paper for a group of learners. Use it with your learners and evaluate how effective it was. What would you change and why?

Making assessment decisions

To know that learning has occurred, some form of assessment must take place. A decision must then be made and a record kept. All decisions should be in accordance with the awarding organisation requirements, and records must be maintained, usually for at least three years. It is quite a responsibility to confirm an achievement (or otherwise) as it can affect your learner's personal and professional development. Your learner may need to pass a qualification to achieve a promotion at work, or they may want to learn a new skill. To make a decision as to whether your learners have achieved, you need to ensure all the required assessment criteria have been met. If you are assessing towards a qualification on the Qualifications and Credit Framework (QCF), successful completion of the assessment criteria will ensure the learning outcomes have been met. You also need to be confident yourself that you understand what you are assessing.

Activity

Ask a colleague if you can observe an assessment activity they are due to carry out. Look at the materials they use, observe how they communicate with their learners, how they reach their decisions, give feedback and complete their records.

Seeing how other assessors plan and assess will help you develop your own skills. Some qualifications may simply be achieved by a pass or a fail, for example a multiple-choice test where learners must achieve seven out of ten for a pass. You would have a list of the correct responses, thus enabling you to mark objectively. You will also have regulations to follow in the event of a fail as to whether your learner can retake the test, and if so, when. Online testing often utilises multiple-choice questions, and instant results can be given. It might not be a good idea to use tests with pass or fail for formative assessments, as negative results could demoralise your learners. However, if you feel they are useful, you could always use pass or refer: any learners with a refer result could have the opportunity to retake the same test, or an alternative one.

If learners are retaking the same test, it's advisable to leave a period of time, for example, seven days, before they take it again. If learners are taking a test that other learners have already attempted, you need to ensure they have not communicated their responses. If learners feel the urge to cheat, they are ultimately only cheating themselves. A bank of questions would be useful, this way you could choose a certain number of questions that will always be different. Computer-generated question papers should automatically choose different questions for different learners. If you are giving any guidance to learners who have been referred, for example, their assignment needs more work, make sure you don't give too much support to the extent that their response is based on your guidance, not their knowledge.

It is harder to remain objective when learners are responding to open questions which do not have clear assessment criteria to follow. Your decisions should always be valid, reliable, fair and ethical.

- Valid – the assessment activity used is appropriate to the subject/qualification being assessed.

- Reliable – if the assessment is carried out again with similar learners, similar results will be achieved.

- Fair – the assessment type is appropriate to all your learners at the required level, is inclusive, i.e. available to all, and differentiates for any particular needs.

- Ethical – the assessment takes into account confidentiality, integrity, safety, security and learner welfare.

Example

Haedish has a group of learners who need to achieve at least eight out of ten to achieve a pass. The questions have been written by a team of staff within the organisation, but no expected responses have been provided. Haedish has been told to use her professional judgement to make a decision, but finds this difficult. She knows her learners are very capable, but they don't always express themselves clearly when writing. She has therefore decided that any learner who achieves a lower mark will not be referred, but will be given the opportunity to respond verbally to her.

In this example, Haedish has made a decision to differentiate for her learners. However she must first check with the other staff that this is acceptable, and if so, they must also be able to offer the same option. This will ensure that all assessors are being fair to all learners.

Peer and self-assessment

Peer assessment involves a learner assessing another learner's progress. Self-assessment involves a learner assessing their own progress. Both methods encourage learners to make decisions about what has been learnt so far, and to reflect on aspects for further development. Your learners will need to fully under-stand the assessment criteria, and how to be analytical and objective with their judgements. Throughout the process of peer and self-assessment, learners can develop skills such as listening, observing and questioning.

Peer assessment advantages are that:

- they can reduce the amount of teacher assessment;

- they increase attention for activities such as peer presentations if feedback has to be given;

- learners are more focused upon the assessment criteria;

- learners may accept comments from peers better than those from the assessor;

- they promote learner and peer interaction and involvement.

Peer assessment limitations include:

- all peers should be involved therefore planning needs to take place as to who will give feedback to whom;

- appropriate conditions and environment are needed;

- assessor needs to confirm each learner's progress and achievements as it might be different from their peer's judgement;

- everyone needs to understand the assessment criteria;

- learners might be subjective and friendly rather than objective with their decisions;

- needs to be carefully managed to ensure no personality conflicts or unjustified comments;

- should be supported with other assessment methods;

- some peers may be anxious, nervous or lack confidence to give feedback.

Self-assessment advantages are that:

- it encourages learners to check their own progress;

- it encourages reflection;

- mistakes can be seen as opportunities;

- it promotes learner involvement and personal responsibility.

Self-assessment limitations include:

- assessor needs to discuss and confirm progress and achievement;

- difficult to be objective when making a decision;

- learners may feel they have achieved more than they actually have;

- learners must fully understand the assessment criteria;

- learners need to be specific about what they have achieved and what they need to do to complete any gaps;

- some learners may lack confidence in their ability to make decisions about their own progress.

Boud (1995) suggested that learning and development will not occur without self-assessment and reflection. This process can promote learner involvement and personal responsibility, however, all learners should be fully aware of the requirements of the qualification and therefore ensure their work is focused upon the assessment criteria. Peer feedback could be written rather than verbal and therefore be anonymous. This would encourage objective opinions as learners will not feel they are betraying their peers. Ground rules should be established to ensure the process is valid and fair.

Examples of peer and self-assessment activities include:

- a written statement of how they could improve their own or peers' work;

- assessing each other's work anonymously and giving written or verbal feedback;

- completing templates or pro-formas;

- giving grades and/or written or verbal feedback regarding own or peer presentations;

- group discussions before collectively agreeing a grade and giving feedback perhaps for a presentation;

- proposing a grade for their own or peers' work;

- suggesting improvements to their own or peers' work.

You may find, when assessing, that your learners haven't achieved everything they should have. When making a decision, you need to base this on all the information or evidence available to you at the time. If your learner has not met all the assessment criteria, you need to give constructive feedback, discuss any inconsistencies and give advice on what they should do next. If your learner disagrees with your decision, they are entitled to follow the appeals or complaints procedures. If you are having difficulty making a decision, discuss this with your line manager or a colleague to obtain a second opinion. You need to be fully confident when making decisions. You are not doing your learners any favours by saying they have achieved something when they haven't. You might also notice skills your learners have that they can use in other situations. It is useful to point out any such transferable skills to help them realise other contexts within which they can work. You may also see other aspects of the qualification requirements demonstrated, in addition to those planned known as naturally occurring evidence. If this is the case, make sure you include it in your decision.

If you are responsible for designing your own assessment activities and materials, you might decide to choose types and methods which are easy to mark. You might not have a lot of time for preparation and marking, therefore the more time you spend preparing something suitable and relevant, the easier the marking will be.

Example

Charlotte sees her group of 18 learners once a week for three hours in a local community centre. She has written some scenarios, which have one correct answer out of three, to formatively assess their progress. As the time she spends with them is used to teach new skills and knowledge, she sets the scenarios as homework. The following week, she begins the session by asking the learners to swop their responses with a partner to mark, as she reads out the correct answers. This way, the marking is done for her, and a group discussion can then take place to clarify any anomalies.

This example works fine for the type of subject and maturity of learners. Experience will enable you to feel more confident with what suits your learners, their level and subject. You might feel uncomfortable trusting your learners to mark one another's, or even their own, work.

You might need to collaborate with other assessors, and make a joint decision regarding your learner's progress. Learners may act differently with other assessors, and you may see things that others hadn't. However, you must always remain objective; you are assessing your learner's competence towards set criteria, not their personality.

If you feel it is difficult to make an objective decision with existing assessment activities, you will need to discuss your concerns with other staff, or with a contact from the awarding organisation. If you are finding it difficult with activities or materials you have designed yourself, you will need to redesign these to make them more specific and unambiguous. If all your learners are achieving everything with ease, perhaps you are not being challenging enough with the tasks you set.

If you are assessing a large amount of work from each learner, perhaps in the form of a portfolio or dissertation, it would be a good idea to have a system of signing this in and out. Your learner will have put a lot of effort into their work, and would like to know that you will take reasonable care with it. When you have made your decision and given feedback, you could ask your learner to sign that they have received it. If your learner was to lose their work, you should have your original assessment records to prove to the awarding organisation that assessment has taken place.

Factors which could influence your judgement and decision

When making a judgement or decision regarding your learner's achievement, you must always follow the awarding organisation's guidelines and assessment strategy, as well as your organisation's quality assurance measures. You must always remain objective and not let certain factors influence you.

- Appeals and complaints – if a learner has made an appeal or complained about a decision you have made, you should not feel you need to pass them if they have not fully met the qualification requirements and assessment criteria. Make sure you follow your organisation's procedures and maintain relevant documents.

- Consistency – are you being fair to all your learners or are you biased towards some learners more than others?

- Methods of assessment – have you used appropriate or alternative methods, for example, professional discussion rather than written questions for a dyslexic learner?

- Plagiarism – have any learners copied work from others or the internet, or not referenced their research adequately? You could type a sentence into a search engine to see if it already exists elsewhere.

- Pressure – do you feel under pressure to pass learners who are borderline, perhaps due to funding measures, retention and achievement targets, inspectors or employer expectations?

- Risk assessments – are any of your learners likely to leave, or do they need extra support for any reason? Don't feel obliged to give too much support, to the extent that your learner's work becomes your own.

- The qualification requirements and assessment criteria – have both you and your learner appropriately interpreted the requirements and assessment criteria?

- Trends – is there a pattern, i.e. are most learners making the same mistakes? If so, it could be that they have misinterpreted something or you have misinformed them. If this is the case, you could summarise these trends and give a copy to your learners, including aspects of good practice to further their development.

- Type of assessment – i.e. formal or informal assessments – you might be more lenient with informal assessments to encourage motivation if the results do not count towards a formal assessment of achievement;

- VACSR – is your learner's evidence valid, authentic, current, sufficient and reliable? How can you ensure their work meets all these points? If you are assessing group work how do you know what each individual has contributed?

If you are in any doubt, you must talk to someone else who is a specialist in your subject area such as your mentor, internal quality assurer or moderator. Samples of your decisions should be checked by your internal quality assurer or moderator to ensure you are assessing correctly and are consistent and fair. However, this usually takes place after you have made a decision and it might be too late if you have made a positive judgement. You will then need to explain to your learner that they have not passed and need to do further work. An external verifier or moderator from the awarding organisation for your subject may also sample your decisions.

Ensuring you choose the right method of assessment to carry out with your learners, and making a decision which is valid, reliable, fair and ethical will help your learners achieve their aim.

Extension Activity

Consider what would influence you when making an assessment decision. Is the assessment criteria explicit, enabling you to be totally objective, or could it be misinterpreted, making it difficult for you to reach a decision? What would you do if you felt under pressure to pass a learner who had not met the assessment criteria?

Summary

In this chapter you have learnt about:

- methods of assessment;
- the role of ICT within assessment;
- questioning;
- making assessment decisions.

Theory focus

References and further information

Boud, D. (1995) *Enhancing Learning Through Self-assessment*. London: Kogan Page.

DfES (2005) *Harnessing Technology: Transforming learning and children's services*. London.

Gravells, A. and Simpson, S. (2009) *Equality and Diversity in the Lifelong Learning Sector*. Exeter: Learning Matters.

Hill, C. (2008) *Teaching with e-learning in the Lifelong Learning Sector* (2nd edn). Exeter: Learning Matters.

JISC (2010) *Effective Assessment in a Digital Age: A guide to technology-enhanced assessment and feedback*. Bristol: JISC Innovation Group, available at: **www.jisc.ac.uk/digiassess**.

LLUK (2007) *Addressing Literacy, Language, Numeracy and ICT Needs in Education and Training: Defining the minimum core of teachers' knowledge, understanding and personal skills*. London: Lifelong Learning UK.

Murphy, P. (1999) *Learners, Learning and Assessment*. London: Paul Chapman Publishing.

Pachler, N, *et al*. (2009) *Scoping a vision for formative e-assessment* (FEASST) JISC.

Race, P., Brown, S. and Smith, B. (2004) *500 Tips on Assessment*. Abingdon: Routledge

Reece, I. and Walker, S. (2007) *Teaching, Training and Learning: A practical guide* (6th edn). Sunderland: Business Education Publishers.

Tummons, J. (2011) *Assessing Learning in the Lifelong Learning Sector* (3rd edn). Exeter: Learning Matters.

Websites

Assessment resources – **www.excellencegateway.org.uk**

Assessment resources – **www.questionmark.co.uk**

ATLS/QTLS – **www.ifl.ac.uk/cpd/qtls-atls**

Efutures (e-assessment regulators) – **www.e-assessment.org.uk**

Peer and self-assessment – **www.nclrc.org/essentials/assessing/peereval.htm**

Plagiarism – **www.plagiarism.org**

Puzzle software – **www.crossword-compiler.com**
      www.educational-software-directory.net/game/puzzle
      http://hotpot.uvic.ca
      www.mathsnet.net

4 RECORDING PROGRESS

Introduction

In this chapter you will learn about:

- providing feedback;
- reviewing learner progress;
- assessment records.

There are activities and examples to help you reflect on the above which will assist your understanding of how to record the progress of learners.

At the end of each section is an extension activity to stretch and challenge your learning further.

This chapter contributes towards the following: scope (S), knowledge (K) and practice (P) aspects of the professional standards (A–F domains) for teachers, tutors and trainers in the Lifelong Learning Sector.

AS7;
AK5.1, AK5.2, AK7.1;
AP1.1, AP2.1, AP2.2, AP5.1, AP7.1;
BS3, BS4;
BK1.2, BK1.3, BK2.2, BK2.5, BK3.2, BK3.5, BK4.1;
BP1.3, BP2.5, BP3.2, BP3.4, BP3.5, BP4.1;
CS2, CS3;
CP1.2, CP3.2, CP3.3, CP3.5, CP4.2;
ES2, ES3, ES4, ES5;
EK2.4, EK3.1, EK4.1, EK4.2, EK5.3;
EP3.1, EP4.1, EP4.2, EP5.1, EP5.2, EP5.5;
FP1.1, FP1.2, FP2.1, FP4.2.

This chapter contributes towards the following Learning and Development Assessor Units:

Unit 1 – 7.1, 7.2
Unit 2 – 2.4, 3.1, 3.2, 3.3
Unit 3 – 2.6, 3.1, 3.2, 3.3

Providing feedback

All learners need to know how they are progressing and what they have achieved at regular points in their learning. Feedback will help encourage, motivate and develop them further. This can be given formally after an assessment, perhaps, in writing, or informally by talking to your learner. When giving feedback in writing, it should always be written on the correct document, not just written on your learner's work, in case they lose it. You can of course make developmental notes on your learner's work, for example to correct spelling errors, or to make annotations to show you have read it. You must keep records of feedback to satisfy internal and external organisation requirements.

Feedback can also be informal and given during a teaching session, to individuals during a review or tutorial, or by telephone, email or another relevant method. When giving feedback, you should always try to be constructive, specific and developmental with what you say. You also need to make sure you are not being ambiguous or vague. You need to be factual regarding the achievements towards the assessment criteria, not just give your opinion. It is important to keep your learners motivated, and what you say can help or hinder their progress and confidence.

Example

All Fatima's learners had passed the required assessment criteria for their first assignment. When marking these, Fatima just wrote 'pass', along with 'good' on each piece of work. Although there were a few spelling and grammatical errors within them all, she did not correct any. She didn't have time to make any comments about how each learner could develop.

While the learners were probably happy they had achieved a pass, they would not be aware what they could improve upon, what was good about it, or that they had made some mistakes. They would therefore continue to make these mistakes, as they would not know differently. It could be that Fatima didn't even spot the mistakes herself. However, you would not want to demoralise your learners by writing too much on their first assignment; a combination of written and oral feedback might be better to retain motivation.

As part of the 2007 Teaching Regulations, teachers need to achieve the minimum core requirements in language, literacy, numeracy and ICT skills. Improving your own skills and knowledge will therefore help support your learners. You can view a copy of the standards via the internet shortcut **http://tinyurl.com/6zmwcg**.

Feedback using constructive comments leads to improved performance – up by 33%. Marking using grades can have a negative effect on learner performance, particularly for low achievers.

Butler (1988, pp. 51–63)

The advantages of giving constructive feedback are:

- it creates opportunities for clarification and discussion;

- it emphasises progress rather than failure;

- it gives your learner confidence;

- it identifies further learning opportunities or action required;

- it motivates your learner;

- your learner knows what they have achieved;

- your learner knows what they need to improve upon or change.

If you are writing feedback to be read by learners at a later date, you need to appreciate that how you write it may not be how they read it. It is easy to interpret words or phrases differently to what is intended; therefore, if you can, read the feedback to them at the time of returning their work. If you don't see your learners regularly, you could mark their work at home and email feedback to them. If so, don't get too personal with this, keep to the facts but be as positive as possible to retain their motivation. If you are giving individual verbal feedback, consider when and where you will do this, so as not to embarrass your learner in any way, and to allow enough time for any questions. Feedback should be a two-way process, allowing a discussion to take place to clarify any points and plan further actions if necessary. Consider your tone of voice and take into account your learner's non-verbal signals. You might give verbal feedback to a group regarding an activity; if so, make sure your feedback is specific to the group, and/or each individual's contributions. Your learners will like to know how they are progressing, and what they need to do to improve or develop further. Simple statements such as 'well done' or 'good' don't tell your learner what was well done or good about their work or how they can improve it. Using your learner's name makes the feedback more personal, and being specific enables your learner to see what they need to do to improve.

Example

Jeremy sees his learners once a fortnight; between times, he marks their assignments and emails informal feedback. A typical email reads: *Paula, you have passed your assignment. I particularly liked the way you compared and contrasted the two styles of writing. Do be careful when proofreading, you tend to use 'were' instead of 'where'. I will return your assignment when I next see you, along with more detailed written feedback.*

This feedback is specific and developmental and will help Jeremy's learners to stay motivated until he next sees them. Giving feedback this way is also a good method of keeping in touch if you don't see your learners frequently, and gives your learners the opportunity to communicate with you if necessary. Emails and written feedback enable you to maintain records, if required, for audit purposes. Feedback can lose its impact if you leave it too long, and learners may think you are not interested in their progress.

Feedback should always be:

- based on facts and not opinions;

- clear, genuine and unambiguous;

- constructive and developmental – giving examples for improvement or further development;

- documented – records must be maintained;

- helpful and supportive;

- honest, specific and detailed regarding what was or wasn't achieved.

Activity

Think of an instance where you have given feedback recently: how did you do this and could you have improved it in any way? What did you find difficult about giving feedback and why?

There could be issues such as not having enough time to write detailed feedback, or perhaps you are not very good with eye contact when giving verbal feedback, or being specific and developmental. Giving constructive feedback comes with practice.

> *If rich feedback is to be given to all learners, then tutors need the time to read and reflect on their assignments, time to write encouraging and stretching comments, and time to discuss these face to face.*

> Coffield (2008, p. 36)

The role of questioning in feedback allows your learner to consider their achievements before you tell them. A good way to start this is to ask your learner how they feel they have done. This gives them the opportunity to realise their own mistakes, or reflect on what they could do differently. You could then build on this through feedback, and discuss what needs to be achieved next.

Having good listening skills will help you engage your learners in a conversation by hearing what they are saying and responding to any questions or concerns. Giving your learners time to talk will encourage them to inform you of things they might not otherwise have said, for example, if something has had an effect upon their progress. Listening for key words will help you focus upon what is being said, for example, *I struggled with the last part of the assignment*. The key word is *struggled* and you could therefore ask a question such as, *What made you struggle?* This would allow a conversation to then take place, giving you the opportunity to help and motivate your learner.

When questioning:

- allow enough time;

- ask open questions, e.g., who, what, when, where, why and how;

- avoid trick questions;

- be aware of your posture, gestures and body language;

- be conscious of your dialect, accent, pitch and tone;

- don't ask more than one question in the same sentence;

- involve everyone if you are talking to a group;

- try not to say *erm, yeah, okay, you know,* or *does that make sense?* (the latter may only gain a *yes* response as learners feel that is what you want to hear);

- use active listening skills;

- use eye contact;

- use learners' names;

- watch your learners' reactions.

Questioning and feedback should always be adapted to the level of your learners. You won't help your learners if you are using higher-level words or jargon, when their level of understanding is lower. You should also be aware of where you give the feedback, in case you are interrupted or in a noisy environment. You should always give feedback in a way which will make it clear how your learner has met the required outcomes, and what they need to do next.

Example

Hanna is working towards the Certificate in Customer Service. She has just been observed by her assessor Geoff, who has also marked her responses to the written questions. Geoff gave her verbal feedback stating: *Hanna, you've done really well and passed all the criteria for the observation and written questions. You dealt with the irate customer in a pleasant and calm way. However, I would recommend you use the customer's name a bit more when speaking with them to appear friendly. You've met all the requirements; we can now sign that unit off and plan for the next one.*

In this example, the assessor was specific, constructive and positive with his feedback; Hanna knew that she had achieved the unit, and what she could do to improve for the future. The use of the word *however* is much better than the word *but*, which sounds negative. The feedback was also worded at the right level for the learner.

Often, the focus of feedback is likely to be on mistakes rather than strengths. If something positive is stated first, any negative comments are more likely to be listened to and acted upon. Starting with a negative point may discourage your learner from listening to anything else that is said.

Peer assessment and feedback can also be useful to develop and motivate learners. However, this should be managed carefully, as you may have some learners who do not get along, and might use the opportunity to demoralise one another. You would need to give advice to your learners as to how to give feedback effectively;

for example, start with something positive, then state what could be improved, and finish on a developmental note. If learner feedback is given skilfully, other learners may consider more what their peers have said than what you have. If you consider peer assessment has a valuable contribution to make to the assessment process, ensure you plan for it, to enable your learners to become accustomed and more proficient at giving it.

Different feedback methods include:

- Descriptive – gives examples of what could be improved and why and is usually formal. Using this method lets you describe *what* your learner has done, *how* they have achieved the required assessment criteria and *what* they can do to progress further.

- Evaluative – usually just a statement such as *well done* or *good*. This method does not offer helpful or constructive advice and is usually informal. It does not give learners the opportunity to know *what* was done well or *how* they could improve.

- Constructive – is specific and focused to confirm your learner's achievement or to give developmental points in a positive and helpful way.

- Destructive – relates to improvements which are needed and is often given in a negative way which could demoralise your learner.

- Objective – clearly relates to specific assessment criteria and what has and has not been met.

- Subjective – is often just a personal opinion and can be biased, for example, if the assessor is friendly with the learner. Feedback might be vague and not based on the assessment criteria.

When giving feedback to learners you need to be aware that it could affect their self-esteem and whether they continue with the programme or not. The quality of feedback received can be a key factor in their progress and the ability to learn new skills. Ongoing constructive feedback which has been carefully thought through is an indication of your interest in your learner and of your intention to help them develop and do well in the future.

When giving feedback:

- own your statements by beginning with the word *I* rather than *you*;

- start with something positive, for example, *I really liked the confident manner in which you delivered your session*;

- be specific about what you have seen, for example, *I felt the way you explained the law of gravity was really interesting due to your knowledge and humour* or *I found the way you explained the law of gravity was rather confusing to me*;

- offer constructive and specific follow on points, for example, *I feel I would have understood it better if you had broken the subject down into smaller stages*;

- end with something positive or developmental, for example, *I enjoyed your session, you had prepared well and came across as very organised and professional. Or I enjoyed your session, however, a handout summarising the key points would be really helpful to refer to in future.*

Being constructive, specific and developmental with what you say, and owning your statements should help your learner focus upon what you are saying, as they will hear how they can improve. If you don't have any constructive, specific or developmental follow-on points then don't create them just for the sake of it. Conversely, if you do have any negative points or criticisms, don't say *my only negative point is...* or *my only criticisms are....* It's much better to replace these words and say *some areas for development could be...* instead.

You will need to find out if your organisation has any specific feedback methods they wish you to use which will ensure a standardised approach across all assessors to all learners.

If assessment decisions count towards the achievement of a qualification, it is crucial you keep your feedback records, along with any action identified, for each learner. Records must always be kept safe and secure; your car boot is not a good idea, nor is a corner of the staffroom. Awarding Organisations expect records to be securely managed.

Extension Activity

Compare and contrast different feedback methods, for example, evaluative and descriptive; constructive and destructive; objective and subjective. Consider the strengths and limitations of each and decide which methods are best suited to your subject along with the reasons why.

Reviewing learner progress

It is important to review learner progress regularly. This gives you the opportunity to discuss on a one-to-one basis how your learners are progressing, what they have achieved, and what they may need to improve or work on in the future. Reviews are a good opportunity to carry out formative assessments in an informal way. They also give your learner the opportunity to discuss any concerns or ask questions they might have been self-conscious about asking in a group situation. The review should be formally documented and signed, and should be carried out at a suitable time during the learning and assessment process. Informal reviews and discussions can take place at any opportune time. Reviewing progress enables you to differentiate effectively, ensuring that the needs of your learners are met, and that they are being challenged to develop to their full potential. It also helps you see when learners are experiencing any difficulties, enabling you to arrange for any necessary support or further training.

Reviewing progress enables you to:

- check skills and knowledge gained from a previous session, before commencing the current session;
- discuss any confidential or sensitive issues;
- discuss achievement of Functional Skills if applicable;

- give constructive and developmental feedback;

- keep a record of what was discussed;

- involve your learners, formally or informally;

- motivate your learners;

- plan for differentiation;

- plan future learning and assessments;

- plan more challenging or creative assessment opportunities;

- provide opportunities for further learning or support;

- review your own contribution to the learning and assessment process;

- revise your scheme of work and session plans;

- revise your strategies for assessment;

- update your learner's assessment plan.

If there is no set procedure, or you are not required to review your learners, it would still be a useful activity if you have the time. When reviewing progress, you should revise or update your learner's assessment plan. The review process should be ongoing until your learner has completed their qualification. Regular reviews can help to keep your learners motivated, make them feel less isolated, and appreciate how they are progressing so far.

The review process should involve:

- arranging a suitable date, time, and location, and confirming these to your learner;

- communicating with anyone else involved in the assessment process prior to the meeting, for example, their supervisor at work;

- obtaining all relevant records relating to your learner, the subject, and the assessments carried out;

- discussing any issues or concerns, progress and achievements so far;

- referring to the previous assessment plan;

- updating the assessment plan with achievements and dates;

- identifying any training needs;

- planning future assessment activities and target dates, (ensuring these are SMART), along with the next review date;

- signing and dating the review record, giving a copy to your learner.

Example

Richard has a group of 12 learners who are attending a weekly evening class from 7 to 9 p.m. for 30 weeks. He has decided to dedicate one session per ten weeks for individual tutorials and reviews. While he is carrying these out, the rest of the group will work on current projects or use the organisation's library or computer facilities. This enables Richard to discuss individual progress, concerns and actions with each learner. It also helps him plan and evaluate his teaching and assessment methods.

Specialist support

At some point, you might have a learner requiring specialist support. Some learners will have needs, barriers or challenges that may affect their attendance and/or achievement. Hopefully you can ascertain these prior to your learners commencing. However, others may occur during the programme and you would need to plan a suitable course of action to help them, or refer them to an appropriate specialist or agency. If you can be proactive and notice potential needs before they become issues, you might be able to alleviate your learner's concerns. Otherwise, you will need to be reactive to the issue and deal with it professionally and sensitively. Examples of potential needs, barriers and challenges might include:

- access to or fear of technology;
- age;
- culture and language differences;
- emotional or psychological problems;
- faith and religion;
- finance;
- hearing or visual impairment;
- hyperactivity;
- lack of confidence, motivation, social skills;
- lack of resources;
- learning difficulties and disabilities;
- limited basic skills such as literacy, numeracy and ICT;
- mental health issues;
- peer pressure;
- personal/work/home circumstances;
- physical, medical, mental or health conditions.

You may feel you can deal with some of these yourself; however, you should always refer your learners to an appropriate specialist or agency if you can't deal with them. Never feel you have to solve any learner problems yourself and don't get personally involved.

If a learner discloses something which is covered by the Disability Discrimination Act (DDA) Part Four (2005), the whole organisation is *deemed to know*. It is therefore important that any issues are communicated to all concerned, and acted upon.

It could be that your learners reveal some personal problems to you. If you don't feel you can help, try to refer them to someone who can, or encourage them to seek advice elsewhere.

Activity

Find out what specialist support is available in your organisation for helping learners, for example counselling. What external agencies could you refer your learners to if necessary?

Always listen to what your learners have to say, without interrupting them; they may not have the opportunity elsewhere to talk to someone about sensitive issues. Always retain confidentiality of information your learners disclose to you, otherwise you could lose their trust and respect. However, you need to know where your boundaries as an assessor stop, and not get involved personally.

You could always review the progress of your learners as a group. At an appropriate time during the programme hold a discussion regarding how they feel they are progressing. This is particularly useful when you need to assess group activities. It could be that some activities do not suit the learning styles of a few learners, therefore not enabling them to fully contribute. Using several different activities could alleviate this, and make the process more interesting. Feedback from group reviews can inform the assessment planning process, and also be a valuable tool to evaluate the programme as a whole.

When assessing and reviewing progress, always try to ensure that the environment meets your learners' basic needs, such as feeling safe and comfortable. This will enable them to feel secure enough to progress further. Maslow (1954) introduced a *Hierarchy of Needs*. These needs represent different levels of motivation and have been adapted by other theorists as time has progressed. The highest level is labelled self-actualising, meaning people are fully functional, possess a healthy personality, and take responsibility for themselves and their actions. Maslow also believed that people should be able to move through these needs to the highest level, providing they are given an education that promotes growth.

The following diagram shows the needs expressed as they might relate to learning.

Figure 4.1 Maslow's hierarchy of needs expressed in educational terms

Ensuring the assessment environment meets your learners' first-level needs will enable them to feel comfortable and secure enough to learn and progress to the higher levels. You will need to appreciate that some learners may not have these lower needs met in their home lives, making it difficult for them to move on to the higher levels in their learning.

Using the correct type of assessment to suit your learners, carrying out careful and appropriate assessment planning and reviewing progress will ensure you are meeting the needs of your learners. You will also make sure your learners are on the right track to achieving a successful result.

Extension Activity

Find out what is involved with the learner review process at your organisation. Is there a particular form you need to complete? Do you have to review all your learners regularly, for example monthly or termly? How can you carry out informal reviews at times to suit both you and your learners?

Assessment records

It is important to keep records, otherwise how would you know what your learners have achieved? You also need to satisfy any organisational, quality assurance, Awarding Organisation and regulatory bodies' audit requirements. This will usually be for a set period, for example three years, and should be the original records, not photocopies or carbon copies. It is fine to give copies to your learners, as it is harder to forge a copy than an original. Sadly, there are learners who do this; therefore keeping the originals will ensure your records are authentic.

When learners submit work, for example an assignment, it is good practice to issue a receipt. If not, a learner might say that they have submitted their work when they haven't.

Keeping full and accurate factual records is also necessary in case one of your learners appeals against an assessment decision. If this happens, don't take it personally – they will be appealing against your decision, not you.

The types of records you might maintain include:

- assessment plan and review;
- assessment tracking sheet and grades;
- feedback report and action plan;
- individual learning plan;
- initial assessment records;
- performance, knowledge and understanding report;
- professional discussion record;
- progress reports;
- records of oral questions;
- standardisation record;
- tutorial reviews.

You might use other documents such as:

- application form;
- authentication statement;
- checklists;
- enrolment form;
- induction record;
- observation report;
- receipts for assignments
- register;
- retention and achievement records;
- unit declarations;
- witness testimony.

There may be a standardised approach to completing the records, for example, the amount of detail which must be written, or whether the records should be completed electronically. Some organisations now use handheld computers to directly input information, and support their learners to produce their work electronically, for example an e-portfolio of evidence.

Some records might be maintained centrally within your organisation using a management information system; these should include:

- learner details: name, address, date of birth, contact information, registration, enrolment, and/or unique learner number (ULN);

- assessor details: name, contact information, curriculum vitae, continuing professional development plans and records;

- schemes of work and session plans for taught programmes;

- internal and external verification/moderation reports;

- records of actions taken from the above reports;

- organisational self-assessment reports;

- awarding organisation syllabus or qualification handbook;

- regulatory and funding guidance;

- evaluation forms and survey results;

- appeals and complaints;

- statistics such as retention and achievement;

- equal opportunities data such as an analysis by ethnic origin, disability, gender and age.

Records can be paper based, electronic, or a mixture of the two. The Data Protection Act (2003) is mandatory for all organisations that hold or process personal data. The Data Protection Act contains eight principles, to ensure that data are:

1. processed fairly and lawfully;

2. obtained and used only for specified and lawful purposes;

3. adequate, relevant and not excessive;

4. accurate and, where necessary, kept up to date;

5. kept for no longer than necessary;

6. processed in accordance with the individual's rights;

7. kept secure;

8. transferred only to countries that offer adequate protection.

Confidentiality should be maintained regarding information. The Freedom of Information Act (2000) gives your learners the opportunity to request to see the information your organisation holds about them. All external stakeholders such as awarding organisation and funding bodies should be aware of your systems of record-keeping as they may need to approve certain records or storage methods. All records should be accurate and legible; if you need to make any amendments, make crossings out rather than use correction fluid. Try to keep on top of your paperwork, even if this is carried out electronically. If you leave it a while, you may forget to note important points. You will need to be organised and have a system; learner records could be stored alphabetically in a filing cabinet, or in separate electronic folders on a computer. If storing electronically, make sure you keep a backup copy in case anything gets accidentally deleted. Other records could be stored by the programme or qualification title, awarding organisation name, etc.

Example

Andrea has a group of 12 learners working towards a Certificate in Health and Social Care qualification. She maintains an A4 lever arch file, which has a tracking sheet at the front to record each learner's completed units. She then has plastic wallets for each learner, filed alphabetically, which contain their assessment plans and reviews, skills and knowledge reports, along with feedback and action plans. She has a separate folder for the awarding organisation standards and blank pro-formas. Each time she completes a pro-forma, she makes a copy to give to her learners.

When completing any records, if signatures are required, these should be obtained as soon as possible after the event if they cannot be signed on the day. Any signatures added later should have the date they were added, rather than the date the form was originally completed. If you are assessing your learners directly, for example by an observation, you will know who they are. If you are assessing work that has been handed to you on a different date, or sent electronically, you will need to ensure it is the work of your learner. Unfortunately, some learners copy or plagiarise the work of others. Sometimes this is deliberate, other times it is due to a lack of knowledge of exactly what was required, or a misunderstanding when referencing quotes. If you feel the work that has been handed to you may not be the actual work of your learner, ask them some questions about it. This will confirm their knowledge, or otherwise. If you feel it isn't their work, you will need to confront them and let them know you will take the matter further. You will then need to inform your line manager or internal verifier/moderator of the situation, explaining to your learner that they have the right to appeal. At this point your learner may confess or they may have what they consider a legitimate excuse. However, you must be certain the work is theirs, otherwise it could be classed as fraud. Your organisation may have anti-plagiarism software you could use before confronting your learner.

Example

Louise and Leanne are sisters, both taking a Certificate in Information Technology, which is assessed by assignments, completed in their own time. When their assessor marked their work, he discovered the answers from both, which had been word-processed, were almost the same. He confronted them individually. Louise insisted the work was her own and had no idea why it looked similar to Leanne's. Leanne became quite upset and admitted to accessing Louise's files without her knowledge. She had been concerned at completing the work within the deadline. In this instance, the assessor credited Louise with the original work, and asked Leanne to re-do the assignment on her own.

It is easier to compare the work of your own learners; however, other assessors in your organisation may also assess the same programme with different learners. In this case, the internal quality assurer/moderator may pick up on issues when they are sampling. It is difficult to check and compare the work of all learners, therefore the importance of authenticity must be stressed to your learners at the commencement of their programme, and continually throughout. Asking learners to sign and date their work is always useful, particularly where this has been prepared on a computer. Some other ways of checking the authenticity of learners' work include:

- syntax, spelling, grammar and punctuation – if you know your learner speaks in a certain way at a certain level, yet their written work does not reflect this;

- work that includes quotes which have not been referenced – without a reference source, this is direct plagiarism and could be a breach of copyright;

- word-processed work that contains different fonts and sizes of text – this shows it could have been copied from the internet, or someone else's electronic file;

- hand-written work that looks different to your learner's normal handwriting, or is not the same style or language as normally used, or word-processed work when they would normally write by hand;

- work that refers to information you haven't taught, or is not relevant to the assessment criteria.

Activity

Find out what your organisation's policy is regarding cheating, copying and plagiarism. Ensure all your learners are aware of it, and encourage them to sign and date all work submitted. This ensures they are taking ownership of their work.

The Copyright, Designs and Patents Act (1988) is the current UK copyright law. Copying the work of others without their permission would infringe the Act. Copyright is where an individual or organisation creates something as an original, and has the right to control the ways in which their work may be used by others.

Normally the person who created the work will own the exclusive rights. However, if the work is produced as part of your employment, for example, if you had produced several handouts or a workbook for your learners, then normally the work will belong to your organisation. Learners may be in breach of this Act if they plagiarise or copy the work of others without making reference to the original author.

If you are assessing the work of learners you might not have met, for example, by e-assessment, it can be very difficult to ensure the authenticity of their work. E-assessment systems often allow contact to take place between the learner and assessor through a website platform. You could communicate in this way, or via email, and then compare the style of writing in the submitted work, to that within the communications.

If you are assessing a programme which is non-accredited, i.e. it is not externally accredited by an awarding organisation, you will need to follow the requirements for recognising and recording progress and achievement in non-accredited learning (RARPA). There are five processes to RARPA.

1. Aims – these should be appropriate to the individual or group of learners.

2. Initial assessment – this should be used to establish each learner's starting point.

3. Identification of appropriately challenging learning objectives – these should be agreed, renegotiated and revised as necessary after formative assessment, and should be appropriate to each learner.

4. Recognition and recording of progress and achievement during the programme – this should include assessor feedback, learner reflection and reviews of progress.

5. End of programme – this includes summative assessment, learner self-assessment and a review of overall progress and achievement. This should be in relation to the learning objectives and any other outcomes achieved during the programme.

If you use the RARPA system, you will need to check what records must be maintained; there may be a standard system for you to follow or you may need to design your own assessment records.

Record-keeping and ensuring the authenticity of your learners' work is of paramount importance. To satisfy all the stakeholders involved in your programme or qualification, you must be able to show a valid audit trail for all your decisions.

Extension Activity

Have a look at the assessment records in Chapter 7. How do they differ to those you are required to use at your organisation? If you are not currently assessing, consider which records you could use for your subject and whether you need to adapt them in any way.

Summary

In this chapter you have learnt about:

- providing feedback;
- reviewing learner progress;
- assessment records.

Theory focus
References and further information

Butler, R. (1988) Enhancing and undermining intrinsic motivation: effects of task-involving and ego-involving evaluation on interest and performance. *British Journal of Educational Psychology* 56 (51–63).

Coffield, F. (2008) *Just Suppose Teaching and Learning Became the First Priority.* London: LSN.

Ofqual (2009) *Authenticity – a guide for teachers.* Coventry: Ofqual.

Websites

Association for Achievement and Improvement through Assessment (AAIA) –
   www.aaia.org.uk/

Data Protection Act (2003) –
   http://regulatorylaw.co.uk/Data_Protection_Act_2003.html

Disability Discrimination Act –
   www.opsi.gov.uk/acts/acts2005/ukpga_ 20050013_en_1

Freedom of Information Act (2000) –
   www.opsi.gov.uk/Acts/acts2000/ukpga_20000036_en_1

Maslow – **www.maslow.com**

Oxford Learning Institute – Giving and receiving feedback –
   www.learning.ox.ac.uk/rsv.php?page=319

Plagiarism – **www.plagiarism.org** and **www.plagiarismadvice.org**

RARPA – **www.rarpatoolkit.com/en/rarpa.asp** and **www.plagiarismadvice.org**

Support for adult learners – **www.direct.gov.uk/adultlearning**

UK Intellectual Property Office – **www.ipo.gov.uk**

5 QUALITY ASSURANCE OF ASSESSMENT

Introduction

In this chapter you will learn about:

- internal quality assurance;

- appeals, complaints and disputes;

- standardisation of practice;

- external quality assurance.

There are activities and examples to help you reflect on the above which will assist your understanding of quality assurance within the assessment process.

A the end of each section is an extension activity to stretch and challenge your learning further.

This chapter contributes towards the following: scope (S), knowledge (K) and practice (P) aspects of the professional standards (A–F domains) for teachers, tutors and trainers in the Lifelong Learning Sector.

AS6, AS7;
AK5.1, AK6.1, AK6.2, AK7.1, AK7.2;
AP4.2, AP5.1, AP5.2, AP6.1, AP7.1, AP7.2;
BS4;
BK2.6;
BP4.1;
CS3;
CK1.1, CK4.1;
CP1.1, CP4.1;
ES2, ES3, ES5;
EK2.4, EK5.1, EK5.2, EK5.3;
EP2.4, EP5.1, EP5.2, EP5.5.

This chapter contributes towards the following Learning and Development Assessor Units:

Unit 1 – 6.1, 6.2, 6.3
Unit 2 – 2.3
Unit 3 – 2.5

Internal quality assurance

All programmes should have a quality assurance system to ensure they are being delivered and assessed fairly, consistently and accurately. Quality assurance should ensure the reliability of assessment decisions, be fair to all learners and uphold the credibility of the assessment process. There are various aspects of quality assurance which will take place internally within your organisation. These include:

- analysing enrolment, retention, achievement and success figures;
- compiling self-assessment reports;
- co-ordinating standardisation activities;
- discussions with learners and witnesses;
- ensuring policies and procedures are regularly reviewed;
- ensuring qualifications are fit for purpose and validated;
- evaluating occupational and assessor competence;
- facilitating appropriate staff development, training and CPD;
- implementing strategies for verification and moderation activities;
- inducting and mentoring new staff, supporting existing staff; carrying out appraisals;
- interpreting qualification requirements correctly;
- maintaining records and audit trails;
- maintaining standards and monitoring risks;
- monitoring appeals, complaints and disputes;
- monitoring learner inductions and progress reviews;
- monitoring questionnaires to learners and responding to feedback;
- observing assessment planning, decisions and feedback;
- preparing for external organisation visits and implementing action points;
- reviewing assessment requirements and strategies;
- sampling assessment plans; decisions and work products;
- setting targets or performance indicators.

You might not be involved with all of the above, but they will have an impact upon your role as an assessor. Your organisation should have a written quality-assurance strategy which you should familiarise yourself with.

It is important to attend team meetings to keep up to date with any changes or developments. If you can't attend a meeting for any reason, make sure you obtain the minutes, and read and act upon any recommendations.

As an assessor, you should be supported by an internal quality assurer/ moderator who will have overall responsibility for the quality of the programme. They will sample your assessed work and give you feedback. They will also ensure you are following Awarding Organisation requirements and are maintaining your professional development. If your job role includes quality assurance of the assessment process you might like to take a relevant qualification such as understanding the Internal Quality Assurance of Assessment Processes and Practice is a theory unit and Internally Assure the Quality of Assessment is a practical unit. Both units will lead to the Level 4 Award in Internal Quality Assurance of Assessment Process and Practice. If you are an assessor, you cannot quality assure your own decisions.

Technology can be used to enhance the quality assurance process by visual or oral recordings of observations and discussions, e-portfolios, online testing and virtual meetings and standardisation activities. This is useful when the quality assurer is located in a different area to the assessor and learners.

If your programme is internally quality assured, and a problem is found when sampling one of your assessment decisions, the quality assurer will give you advice as to how you can put things right with your learner. If your programme is moderated and a problem is found, all learners in your group will need to be reassessed.

Example

Ewan had assessed his group of 12 learners for a Literacy qualification. When the internal moderator, Sheila, sampled two of his marked assignments, she noticed one of the questions had not been fully answered by both learners, yet Ewan had awarded a pass. When Sheila discussed this with Ewan, he realised he had not covered this topic fully with his learners. He therefore delivered the topic correctly the next time he had his group. All learners then had to resubmit their assignment for reassessment.

In this situation, the internal moderator was able to help the assessor, and ultimately his learners. If internal moderation had not taken place, the learners would have achieved a qualification, without successfully achieving all the assessment criteria. If the certificates had been claimed from the awarding organisation, then this could be classed as fraud.

Whether you assess a vocational or an academic subject, your assessment practice will be quality assured in line with a Code of Practice, and/or guidelines and regulations published by the relevant awarding organisation. They will want to ensure you are maintaining the integrity of their name.

Activity

Locate a copy of the awarding organisation's Code of Practice relevant to your subject together with any other requirements for quality assuring the programme you assess. Look at these to make sure you are complying. If you are unsure of any aspect, discuss this with your internal quality assurer/moderator.

There are other external bodies that will advise and monitor quality assurance; these will depend upon which area of the United Kingdom you are working in and whether your organisation receives external funding. They include:

- funding agencies;

- local authority (LA);

- Office for Standards in Education, Children's Services and Skills (Ofsted);

- Office of the Qualifications and Examinations Regulator (Ofqual).

Sector Skills Councils (SSC) and Standards Setting Bodies (SSB) work with employers and partners to develop the standards for the qualifications you might be assessing. Any revisions to the standards will be notified via their website and you can also obtain details regarding the assessment and quality assurance strategies.

Internal quality assurance is crucial to the integrity of the qualification, and the reputation of your organisation.

Extension Activity

Access the Sector Skills website for your particular subject. You can find out their details via www.sscalliance.org. Have a look at the guidance they give for assessing and quality assuring your subject and check when the standards are next due for review. Check that the quality systems within your organisation ensure that all the requirements can be met. If the standards are due for review fairly soon, find out how you can participate.

Appeals, complaints and disputes

At some point during the assessment process, a learner may wish to appeal against one of your decisions, have a complaint, or dispute a grade you have given them. At the induction stage, you should have given your learners information that would enable them to follow your organisation's procedures. Information could also be displayed on noticeboards, in the learner handbook, or be available via your organisation's intranet. Learners will need to know who they can go to, and that their issue will be followed up.

Some organisations will provide a pro-forma for learners to use, which ensures all the required details are obtained, or encourage an informal discussion first. Statistics should be maintained regarding all appeals and complaints; these will help your organisation when reviewing their policies and procedures, and should be provided to relevant external bodies if requested.

Having a climate of respect and honesty can lead to issues being dealt with informally, rather than procedures having to be followed which can be upsetting for both parties concerned.

Complaints may be made against something you have or have not done. If your learner has a complaint, they might not feel confident to discuss it directly with you, but go to a third party.

Example

Jonas had received a pass from his assessor, Chika, for his recent assignment. He felt he had met the criteria for a distinction, but didn't discuss this with his assessor. He complained to another assessor, who informed Chika. At the next session, Chika asked Jonas if he agreed with the grade he received; he said he did.

In this situation, Jonas felt he deserved a higher grade, and complained to a third party, but when given the opportunity to discuss it, he said he agreed with it. This could be because there was a personality clash between the assessor and learner, or he really did agree with the grade, and just wanted to complain for the sake of it. If this happens to you, ask a colleague, or your internal verifier/moderator, to reassess the work. This will confirm whether or not you are correct, and if not, your learner should achieve the revised grade.

A complaint is often about a situation or a person, whereas an appeal or a dispute is about achievement. Learners who complain should be able to do so without fear of recrimination. Confidentiality should be maintained where possible to ensure an impartial outcome. If any of your learners do have an appeal, complaint or dispute, this should not affect the way you or other learners or staff treat them. The outcome should not jeopardise your learner's current or future achievements. You should always remain professional in your role, to promote a positive assessment experience for all your learners.

Extension Activity

Locate read and summarise your organisation's policies and procedures for appeals, complaints and disputes in your particular subject area. Compare these with the requirements of your awarding organisation (if applicable).

Standardisation of practice

Standardisation ensures consistency and fairness of all assessment decisions. You may have to standardise your decisions with other assessors, particularly where more than one assessor is involved with the same subject. It is also a chance to ensure all assessors are interpreting the qualification requirements and assessment criteria correctly, and completing records appropriately. Attending a standardisation event will give you the opportunity to share good practice and compare your assessment decisions with your colleagues, by looking at their assessed work and vice versa. You could also standardise your practice virtually or electronically by reviewing standards or documents online. Even if you don't learn anything new, it will confirm you are doing things right. Standardisation events are not team meetings; the latter are to discuss issues relating to the management of the programme, for example, awarding organisation updates, targets, success rates and learner issues.

Example

Lukas was a new assessor, and was not very familiar with the revised standards of the qualification he was due to assess. The full team of assessors met once a fortnight to discuss the content of each unit, to ensure they were all interpreting it correctly. At this meeting, they would also swop units they had assessed, enabling the team to see how assessments had been planned, carried out and documented. This prompted a discussion which ensured all the assessors could standardise their practice. Records were kept which could be referred to in case of a query, which greatly helped Lukas understand the standards.

The benefits of standardisation are:

- a contribution to continuing professional development;
- accountability to external bodies;
- all assessment decisions are fair for all learners;
- an opportunity to discuss new standards;
- clearly defined roles and responsibilities;
- compliance with Awarding Organisations' Codes of Practice;
- confirming your own practice;
- consistency and fairness of judgements and decisions;
- empowerment of assessors to take responsibility;
- ensuring the assessment strategy is followed;
- sharing good practice;
- spotting trends or inconsistencies;
- succession planning if assessors are due to leave;
- to give an audit trail of aspects standardised;
- to give assessors time to formally meet to discuss assessments;
- to meet quality assurance requirements;
- to set action plans for the development of systems and staff.

If you assess an academic qualification, you might use the term *double marking* rather than standardisation. This enables different assessors to mark one another's assessed work, to ensure the correct grade has been given. This might take place blindly, i.e. you don't get to see the original grade. Having a marking scheme or expected answers will help you reach a fair decision. If standardisation was not carried out, assessment activities would not be fair to all learners.

If you assess a vocational qualification, you might carry out three observations with your learners, and give them a written test, whereas another assessor might only carry out one observation and ask some questions orally. There are times when an individual learner's needs should be taken into account, which will lead to a difference in assessment activities. However, all learners should be entitled to the same assessment experience, no matter which assessor they are allocated to.

> *Standardised summative assessments, marked in the same way for everyone, are necessary for any modern society, which aspires to fairness and justice for its citizens.*
>
> Wolf (2008, p. 19)

It's important to keep up to date with any changes to qualification standards. Awarding organisations issue regular updates, either by hard copy or electronically. Once you receive these, you need to discuss the content with your colleagues to ensure you all interpret them the same way. It would prove useful to maintain minutes of meetings reflecting any changes and updates.

Extension Activity

Look at the qualification standardisation pro-forma in Chapter 7. Does your organisation use something similar? If not, use this form next time to ensure you are standardising your judgements with other assessors. What other standardisation activities would you carry out and why?

External quality assurance

If your qualification is externally quality assured, a member of the relevant awarding organisation will visit to ensure you are compliant with their requirements, assessment and quality assurance strategies. They will be known as an external verifier or moderator, or external quality consultant.

Never be concerned about making contact with them. They are there to help ensure you assess the qualification correctly, and would not want you to do anything that contravenes regulations. However, your organisation may prefer you to make contact through your internal quality assurer/moderator, to ensure they are aware of the advice and support given, and to share this with the team.

The external verifier or moderator will:

- check that claims for certification are authentic, valid and supported by auditable records;

- complete a report and identify any relevant action;

- confirm that assessments are conducted by appropriately qualified staff;

- confirm that organisations have carried out any previous corrective actions;

- ensure compliance with the approval criteria;

- ensure procedures are followed, including access to fair assessment and appeals;

- ensure that national standards are being consistently maintained;

- follow an audit trail through assessment and verification/moderation records;

- give advice and support regarding the interpretation of standards;

- observe assessment and verification/moderation activities;

- read minutes of meetings and check standardisation records;

- recommend actions for non-compliance if requirements are not met;

- report any malpractice;

- sample assessment decisions to confirm that they are authentic and valid;

- talk to learners and others involved in the assessment process.

Prior to their visit, you will need to liaise with your internal quality assurer/moderator to ensure all the external requirements have been met, and that the requested sample of work is available. The external verifier/moderator may want to observe you with your learners, check your records, and sample your assessed work.

After a visit, your internal verifier/moderator should hold a meeting with the team to discuss any issues and action points. You should receive a copy of the minutes, and carry out any action points that have been allocated to you. The external verifier/moderator should then be informed when all the actions have been completed.

Always make sure you are assessing according to all the relevant regulations and guidelines, if you are in any doubt, talk to your internal verifier/moderator or person responsible for quality assurance within your organisation.

Extension Activity

Obtain the name and contact details of the external verifier/moderator who has been allocated for your qualification. Find out when they are next due to visit and read their last report beforehand. Check what action points or comments they stated and ensure that you are following them.

Summary

In this chapter you have learnt about:

- internal quality assurance;

- appeals, complaints and disputes;

- standardisation of practice;
- external quality assurance.

Theory focus
References and further information

Wolf, A. (2008) Looking for the best result, in *Make the Grade,* summer 2008, Institute of Educational Assessors. **www.ioea.org.uk**

Wood, J. and Dickinson, J. (2011) *Quality Assurance and Evaluation in the Lifelong Learning Sector.* Exeter: Learning Matters.

Websites

Ofqual – **www.ofqual.gov.uk**
Ofsted – **www.ofsted.gov.uk**
QAA – **www.qaa.ac.uk**
Sector Skills Councils – **www.sscalliance.org**

Introduction

In this chapter you will learn about:

- learner evaluation;

- programme evaluation;

- self-evaluation;

- continuing professional development.

There are activities and examples to help you reflect on the above which will assist your understanding of evaluation, and continuing professional development (CPD).

At the end of each section is an extension activity to stretch and challenge your learning further.

This chapter contributes towards the following: scope (S), knowledge (K) and practice (P) aspects of the professional standards (A–F domains) for teachers, tutors and trainers in the Lifelong Learning Sector.

AS4, AS5, AK1.1, AK2.1, AK4.2, AK4.3, AK5.1, AK7.3, AP3.1, AP4.2, AP4.3, AP5.1, AP5.2, AP7.2, AP7.3;
BK2.6, BP2.6, BP3.3, BP3.4 BP5.2;
CS1, CS3, CK4.1, CP1.1, CP3.4, CP4.1;
DS1, DS2, DS3, DK1.1, DK3.1, DK3.2, DP2.1, DP3.1, DP3.2;
ES4, ES5, EK2.1, EK2.2, EK2.4, EK4.1, EK4.2, EK5.1, EK5.3, EP1.1, EP2.4, EP3.1, EP4.1, EP4.2, EP5.1, EP5.2, EP5.5;
FS3, FK3.1, FK4.2.

This chapter contributes towards the following Learning and Development Assessor Units:

Unit 1 – 7.2, 8.4
Unit 2 – 4.3, 4.4
Unit 3 – 4.3, 4.4

Learner evaluation

Evaluation is not another term for *assessment*; evaluation is a way of obtaining feedback to improve your own performance, the support you give your learners, and to ensure the assessment processes used are effective, valid and reliable. Information gained from evaluations should lead to an improvement for learners, yourself and your organisation. Never assume everything is going well just because you think it is. Encouraging learners to talk to you about anything you can do to help them, or things you can change to support their learning, will help build a climate of trust and respect. Learners may be embarrassed to talk in front of their peers, but unless you know of any issues that may affect them, you can't fully support them.

As well as encouraging informal feedback and discussions, you can gain formal feedback from your learners by using surveys and questionnaires. Your organisation may have standard ones you are required to use, or you could design your own. Always build time into your session for this to take place, otherwise your learners will take away the questionnaire and may forget to return it. Alternatively, questionnaires could be completed online and analysed automatically.

When designing questionnaires, you need to be careful of the type of questions you are using, and consider why you are asking them. Don't just ask questions for the sake of issuing a questionnaire; consider what you really want to find out. When writing questions, gauge the language and level to suit your learners. Will your questions be closed, i.e. a question only requiring a *yes* or *no* answer, will they be multiple choice, enabling your learner to choose one or more responses to a question, or will they be open, leading to detailed responses?

Example

Was the assessment activity as you expected? YES/NO

This closed question would not help you to understand what it was that your learner expected, or even what their expectations were. This would be better phrased: **How did the assessment activity meet your expectations?** *This open question encourages your learner to answer in detail and gives you something to act on.*

If you would rather use questions with *yes/no* responses, you could ask a further question to enable your learner to elaborate on why they answered *yes* or *no*.

Example

Was the assessment activity as you expected? YES/NO
Why was this?

This enables your learner to expand on their response, and gives you more information.

If you use closed or multiple-choice questions, you can add up how many responses you gained to give you quantitative data. Other responses will give you qualitative data. Quantitative data are useful for obtaining statistics, but will not give you much information to help you improve specific aspects of your programme. Although you can add up the responses quickly from quantitative data, qualitative data are more useful. You might find it best to use a mixture of open and closed questions. When designing questionnaires, use the KISS method – *Keep it Short and Simple*. Don't overcomplicate your questions, e.g. by asking two questions in one sentence, or make the questionnaire so long that learners will not want to complete it. Inform your learners why you are asking them to complete the questionnaire and what the information will be used for. Always make sure you follow up their responses, and inform your learners of the results and actions to be taken, otherwise the evaluation process is meaningless.

You can also gain learner feedback after carrying out an assessment, for example, during a one-to-one conversation, or a group discussion. You may need to update or amend your learner's assessment plan, or revise the assessment process or any materials/resources used as a result. You might find out that the method of assessment you have been using, for example projects and quizzes, is not challenging enough for your learner. They might prefer more formal methods such as a written test.

Some learners might not feel comfortable giving verbal feedback, and you may not have the opportunity to issue a questionnaire. A way to get around this could be to encourage anonymous feedback, perhaps by using a feedback box. This is similar to a suggestion box, but you could encourage compliments as well as criticisms or complaints. It doesn't have to be a box, it could be a large envelope pinned to a noticeboard, or a pigeonhole somewhere. If you do use this method, give your learners a summary of the information you have received and what you have acted upon. If learners take the time to give you feedback, you should also take the time to respond to it.

Obtaining the views of your learners will greatly assist you when reflecting upon your role as an assessor. You could ask your learners directly after an assessment activity how they felt the process was. However, some learners might feel confident enough to tell you, but others might not. When evaluating your own practice, you need to consider the views of your learners and others in order to improve. How you do this will depend upon the type of feedback you have obtained and how useful it will be. A survey might have ascertained that most learners felt the initial assessment could be improved, for example, a computerised learning styles' test rather than a paper-based one. You might have obtained feedback from an individual learner that their assessment plan had unrealistic target dates. In this case, you could renegotiate the plan with more suitable dates. Feedback from your learners might impact upon your role by enlightening you to other aspects, for example, the types of questions used in an assignment were too complex, some activities may not have been challenging enough, or a multiple-choice test confused a dyslexic learner as they mistook a *b* for a *d*. You will need to ensure the activities you used to assess knowledge, skills and attitudes were valid and reliable, and that you only assessed the criteria you were meant to assess. You will also need to evaluate if the assessment types and methods you used were successful. You will need to ask yourself if you assessed fairly, or if you had a favourite learner who you gave more attention, or were lenient with for any reason. The views of your learners and others should have an impact upon your own role by helping you improve the assessment experience for your learners.

Extension Activity

Design a short questionnaire that you could use with your learners. This could be given to a group or an individual. Consider the types of questions you will ask, based upon the information you need. If possible, use it, analyse the results and recommend improvements to be made based on these.

Searching the internet will give you lots of ideas regarding questionnaire design. You could create an online questionnaire rather than a paper-based one.

Programme evaluation

Whatever type of programme you are assessing, it is important to evaluate the process to ensure learning has been successful, and to inform future programme planning. It will also help you realise how effective you were and what you could improve in the future. It may help you identify any problem areas, enabling you to do things differently next time. Evaluating the programme will include analysing the results of questionnaires from your learners, as well as obtaining feedback from colleagues, management, employers, workplace supervisors, or inspectors and verifiers who may also be involved. Part of the quality-assurance process will involve you being observed at some point either assessing learners or giving feedback.

Activity

If you have been observed lately, look at the feedback on the observation report. Was there anything identified that needed improving or changing; if so, have you done this?

If you haven't been observed, ask a colleague or your mentor to observe you during the assessment process to gain constructive feedback.

Always make sure you do something with the feedback you receive, to help improve your assessment practice, and your learners' experiences in the future. You may not agree with some of the feedback. Don't take it personally, but learn from the experience of your observer. They may see things you didn't realise or appreciate. You could always ask if you could observe them, or another more experienced colleague, to help improve your practice.

If you are assessing employees in their work environment, you may like to obtain feedback from their employers to check that their newly acquired skills and knowledge have been put into practice successfully. If the employees are working towards a qualification, the employer may be paying for this and will want to know how they are progressing. If some of the employees did not achieve, the employer will want to know why. You would need to make an evaluation as to whether it was your planning and assessment methods or other factors that led to this. If you are giving feedback to others in the work environment, always be tactful and diplomatic, and follow organisational procedures regarding confidentiality.

Example

Ravi had assessed Paul for a unit of the Diploma in Motor Vehicle Maintenance. After the assessment, Ravi didn't give Paul any feedback, but spoke directly to his employer about his progress. He informed the employer that Paul would never achieve the qualification and he didn't know why he had been employed in that trade in the first place.

In this instance, Ravi should have discussed the result of the assessment with Paul first: there could have been a legitimate reason as to why he hadn't performed well. If the employer wanted to be kept informed of Paul's progress, Ravi could have spoken to him in a more tactful way, explaining why Paul hadn't achieved, and planning a date for a further assessment. Learners need to be able to trust their assessors and to feel comfortable talking to them.

Your organisation may carry out an evaluation of your programme, perhaps to decide if it should be offered again in the future. They may make this decision based upon the number of learners recruited to the programme, their attendance patterns and whether they obtained a qualification at the end.

You may have to write a programme report which your organisation will use as a basis to make a decision about the future. This report may also include retention and achievement statistics. If the targets are not met, your programme may not be offered again. Some programmes might only be offered again if external funding can be obtained.

Activity

Find out how the programmes you assess are funded. Do your learners or their employers pay, do they receive a grant, or does your organisation fund it? Find out the name of the external funding agency (if applicable) and the requirements they impose upon your organisation, for example, target dates and learner numbers. How do you feel this will affect the quality of the assessment and quality assurance processes?

Knowing how your programme is funded will help you realise the constraints and pressures your learners and your organisation may be under. If your learners do not achieve within the designated time period, you may need to carry out further assessments which will impact on the overall success rates, the funding received, and also add further work for yourself as you may need to carry out more assessments.

If you assess a programme which requires grades to be given to learners, you will need to analyse data regarding their achievements. The grades could be expressed as:

- 1, 2, 3, 4, 5;

- A, B, C, D, E;

- competent/not yet competent;

- distinction, credit, pass, fail;

- pass, refer, fail;

- percentages, e.g. 80%;

- satisfactory, good, outstanding.

Once you have analysed your data, you will need to consider what has contributed towards them. For example, if you had a group of 30 learners who all achieved an A grade, was this due to your excellent teaching and assessing, the skills and knowledge of your learners, or by being too lenient with your grades when marking? If you had a group of 15 learners who all failed an assignment, you could ask yourself the same questions. However, it could be that the assignment questions were worded in a confusing way, or you had given the assignment too early in the programme. If most of your group averaged a grade of 50%, whereas a colleague's group's averaged 80%, was this because you had given your learners misleading or ambiguous information relating to that topic? Asking yourself these questions will help you ascertain if you are producing assessments that are fit for purpose, and if not, you will need to do something about it, for example, amending your teaching or assessment methods, rewording questions or redesigning assessment activities.

Your organisation might employ new assessors and you may be asked to mentor and support them. They should be given an induction to the assessment policy and procedures, all relevant paperwork and systems, the awarding organisation requirements as well as your organisational requirements. If assessors are leaving, there should be a system of succession planning, to allow time for a successful handover, and any relevant training to take place. Usually, the awarding organisation will need to be informed of any new staff to ensure that they are suitably qualified.

You may need to evaluate the resources you use, for example handouts, to ensure they are inclusive, promote equality and engage with diversity. You will also need to evaluate whether the assessment types and methods you used were successful. You will need to ensure the activities you used to assess knowledge, skills and understanding were valid and reliable, and that you only assessed the criteria you were meant to assess. You will need to ask yourself if you assessed fairly, or if you had a favourite learner to whom you gave more attention, or were lenient with for any reason.

Example

Lorraine had taken a group of 24 learners for a programme which had marking criteria of pass, refer and fail for three assignments. The qualification was not externally accredited, i.e. the organisation issued their own certificates, but marking guidance had been agreed by the programme team. Lorraine had one particular learner who had problems at home, and already had two assignments referred. Both assignments had been resubmitted by the learner who subsequently achieved a pass, only due to Lorraine's extra support. The third assignment should have been another refer, but Lorraine gave a pass, as she did not want to demoralise her learner any more, nor be seen to give him more support.

In this instance, Lorraine had not been fair to the group, as she had given extra support to one particular learner. If all the learners had struggled, she could evaluate why this was: perhaps the assignment instructions were not clear. She should not have given a grade of *pass* if it should have been *refer*, as this is an invalid result. It is also not a reliable result as all the learners' responses are not being assessed consistently. However, there will be instances when a particular learner may require extra support, due to their individual needs but you should always remain objective with your decisions.

You will also need to ensure you are giving feedback which is developmental to your learner, advising and guiding them where and how they can improve and not giving them support to the extent that their work becomes mainly yours.

Standardising your practice with other assessors, verification and moderation will help ensure you are assessing fairly and consistently.

Extension Activity

Find out how your programme or qualification will be evaluated within your organisation. How will you be involved with this and when will it take place? What factors will contribute towards the decision as to whether the programme or qualification will be offered again?

Self-evaluation

Self-evaluation involves continually reflecting upon your own practice. You need to evaluate yourself, to ensure you are carrying out your role effectively. When evaluating your own practice, you need to consider how your own behaviour has impacted upon your learners and what you could do to improve as an assessor. You also need to evaluate the assessment methods you have used. If they are not a requirement of an awarding organisation, you should be able to amend them if necessary.

Activity

Think about the last assessment activity you carried out with your learners. Did it go as planned? If not, why not? What could you do to put this right? If it went well, was it challenging enough or too easy?

It could be that you didn't have enough time to plan the assessment in advance, therefore not giving enough information to your learners. Or you might have rushed the assessment activity due to time constraints, or couldn't complete the paperwork fully. After each assessment activity you carry out, evaluate how you feel it went, what was good about it and what could be improved.

A straightforward method of reflection is to have the *experience*, then *describe it*, *analyse it* and *revise it* (EDAR). This method should help you think about what has happened and then consider ways of changing and/or improving it.

Experience → *Describe* → *Analyse* → *Revise*

EDAR (Gravells, 2008)

- *Experience* – a significant event or incident you would like to change or improve.

- *Describe* – aspects such as who was involved, what happened, when it happened and *where* it happened.

- *Analyse* – consider the experience deeper and ask yourself how it happened and why it happened.

- *Revise* – think about how you would do it differently if it happened again and then try this out if you have the opportunity.

A way of getting in the habit of reflective practice is to complete an ongoing journal; however, try not to write it like a diary with a description of events, but use EDAR to reflect upon the event.

You may see your own skills developing, for example giving effective, developmental and constructive feedback.

Reflection should become a habit. If you are not able to write a reflective journal, mentally run through the EDAR points in your head when you have time. As you become more experienced at reflective practice, you will progress from thoughts of *I should have let my learner realise their own mistake before telling them* to aspects of more significance to your professional role as an assessor. You may realise you need further training or support in some areas before feeling confident to make changes.

Keeping a reflective learning journal will help you plan aspects for your continuing professional development (CPD).

Kirkpatrick (2006) originally proposed the *four levels of evaluation model* in 1959, which measure:

- reaction, i.e. what the learners thought and felt about the experience;

- learning, i.e. increased knowledge, skills and attitudes;

- behaviour, i.e. improved performance and competence;

- results, i.e. the effects on the environment, other people and the organisation.

Asking your learners questions based on reaction, learning, behaviour and results should empower them to take responsibility for their learning, assessment and achievement. Ultimately their change in behaviour will benefit not only themselves, but the organisation they work for and the people they work with. The impact from this type of evaluation will also help you improve your own behaviour as an assessor, as well as for your learners and your organisation. Evaluation isn't just about obtaining feedback to find out if your learners have had a good experience with you. It's about how those experiences have influenced their knowledge, skills and attitudes not only to improve their behaviour, but to benefit all concerned.

Extension Activity

Use the reflective learning journal pro-forma in Chapter 7 to reflect upon your last assessment activity, using EDAR to help you. Did you have any issues or problems during the assessment process? If you did, what could you do to stop this happening again? If you have a mentor, discuss your experience with them. You might like to create a SWOT analysis (strengths, weaknesses, opportunities and threats) regarding your role as an assessor.

Continuing professional development

Initial Professional Development (IPD) begins if you are not already qualified or are currently working towards an assessor qualification. Continuing Professional Development (CPD) should be carried out regularly, to maintain your occupational competence not only as an assessor but also regarding your subject and advances in technology.

As a professional, you need to continually update your skills and knowledge. This knowledge relates not only to your subject specialism, but assessment methods, the types of learners you will be assessing, and relevant organisational and national policies. CPD can be formal or informal, planned well in advance or be opportunistic, but it should have a real impact upon your job role and lead to an improvement in your practice as an assessor.

CPD is more than just attending events; it is also using critical reflection regarding your experiences which result in your development as an assessor. Shadowing colleagues, for example, observing how they assess, joining professional associations, and internet research will all help your development.

> *Reflection is not simply something that you should do to meet the criteria once a development activity has been completed; it is integral to the whole process of professional growth.*
>
> Hitching (2008, p.13)

Opportunities for continuing professional development include:

- attending events, meetings, standardisation activities and training programmes;

- e-learning activities;

- evaluating feedback from peers and learners;

- improving own skills such as literacy or numeracy;

- membership of professional associations or committees;

- observing and shadowing colleagues;

- researching developments or changes to your subject and/or relevant legislation;

- self-reflection;

- studying for relevant qualifications;

- subscribing to and reading relevant journals and websites;

- visiting other organisations;

- voluntary work;

- work experience placements;

- writing or reviewing books and articles.

You can update your CPD record via the IfL Reflect website (**www.ifl.ac.uk**); by now you should have registered as a member and you will have access to a wealth of information regarding ways to maintain your CPD.

When planning your CPD, it is a good idea to complete a personal development plan. This enables you to consider your development needs and the best way to achieve them which should relate directly to your job role or subject specialism.

You will probably partake in an appraisal system at your organisation. This is a valuable opportunity to discuss your learning and any training or support you may need in the future. Always keep a copy of any documentation relating to your training and CPD, as you may need to provide this to funding, awarding organisation or regulatory bodies if requested.

Having the support of your organisation will help you decide what is relevant to your development as an assessor, and your job role.

The practice of assessment has been recognised as a professional activity by the granting of Chartered Status to the Institute of Educational Assessors (CIEA). Their aim is to improve the quality of assessment in schools and colleges by working with educational assessors to develop their knowledge, understanding and capability in all aspects of educational testing and assessment. You can access their standards by visiting their website (**www.ciea.org.uk**).

Reflecting upon your own assessment practice, taking account of feedback from learners and colleagues, evaluating your practice and maintaining your professional development, will enable you to become a more effective assessor.

Extension Activity

Consider what CPD you feel is relevant, for example, improving your literacy or numeracy skills. Use the personal development plan pro-forma in Chapter 7 to formalise your requirements. Complete the continuing professional development record with recent CPD activities. If you have not already registered with the IFL, do this now and then upload your CPD details to Reflect.

Summary

In this chapter you have learnt about:

- learner evaluation;

- programme evaluation;

- self-evaluation;

- continuing professional development.

Theory focus

References and further information

Cohen, L., Manion, L. and Morrison, K. (2007) *Research Methods in Education.* London: Routledge.

Denscombe, M. (2002) *Ground Rules for Good Research.* Buckingham Open University Press.

Hitching, J. (2008) *Maintaining Your Licence to Practise.* Exeter: Learning Matters.

Kirkpatrick, D. and Kirkpatrick, J. (2006) *Evaluating Training Programs: The Four Levels* (3rd edn) San Francisco: Berrett-Koehler.

Tummons, J. (2011) *Assessing Learning in the Lifelong Learning Sector* (3rd edn). Exeter: Learning Matters.

Wallace, S. and Gravells, J. (2007) *Mentoring.* Exeter: Learning Matters.

Wood, J. and Dickinson, J. (2011) *Quality Assurance and Evaluation in the Lifelong Learning Sector.* Exeter: Learning Matters.

Websites

Chartered Institute of Educational Assessors – **www.ciea.org.uk**
Institute for Learning – **www.ifl.ac.uk**

7 SAMPLE DOCUMENTATION

This chapter contains sample documents referred to within the previous chapters, which you may like to use in preparation for, or as part of, your assessment role. They are examples only, and can be adapted to suit your own requirements. If you are currently assessing, your organisation will already have certain documents they will require you to use, which may differ from these.

The following documents are also available from the publisher's website: **www.learning matters.co.uk**.

- Initial assessment record

- Assessment plan and review

- Performance, knowledge and understanding report

- Feedback record and action plan

- Assessment tracking sheet

- Standardisation record

- Personal development plan

- Continuing professional development record

- Reflective learning journal

Initial assessment record

Learner: **Date:**

Programme/Qualification: **Venue:**

What relevant experience do you have?		
What relevant qualifications do you have?		
Have you completed a learning styles questionnaire? If YES, what is your preferred style of learning?	YES/NO	
Do you have any particular learning needs or requirements? If YES, please state, or talk to your assessor in confidence.	YES/NO	
Are you confident at using a computer? If YES, what experience or qualifications do you have?	YES/NO	Skills scan results: ICT:
Do you feel you have a good command of written/ spoken English?	YES/NO	Skills scan results: Literacy:
Do you feel your numeracy skills need improving?	YES/NO	Skills scan results: Numeracy:
Why have you decided to take this programme/ qualification (*continue overleaf*)		

An assessment plan should now be agreed.

Signed (assessor):   Signed (learner):

Assessment plan and review

Learner: **Assessor:**

Qualification and level: **Unique learner number:**

Date commenced: **Expected completion date:**

Date	Aspect of qualification (unit/learning outcome or assessment criteria)	Date achieved	Assessment details **Planning** – methods of assessment, activities and SMART targets **Review** – revisions to plan, achievements and issues discussed	Target/ review date	Agreed by (assessor and learner to sign)

This document is an ongoing record of learner progress.

Separate records must be completed for the assessment of performance, knowledge and understanding, as well as a feedback record and action plan.

Countersignature and date (if required):

Performance, knowledge and understanding report

Learner: **Assessor:**

Qualification: **Level:**

Date assessed: **Date feedback given:**

Aspect of qualification assessed (unit, learning outcome or assessment criteria) **formative/summative**	**Performance** – observation of skills: state what was observed and how the aspects were achieved in relation to the qualification **Knowledge** – note questions and responses, results of RPL/tests & activities, professional discussion points etc
Assessment decision:	valid ☐ authentic ☐ current ☐ sufficient ☐ reliable ☐ achieved/not yet achieved YES/NO further action required? YES/NO feedback record and action plan completed? YES/NO

Signed (assessor):   Signed (learner):

Countersignature and date (if required):

Feedback record and action plan

Learner: **Assessor:**

Qualification: **Level:**

Aspect of qualification assessed	Feedback	Action required (assessment plan to be updated)	Target date

Signed (assessor):   Date:

Signed (learner):   Date:

Countersignature and date (if required):

Assessment tracking sheet

Assessor:

Qualification and level:

Learners:

Aspect of qualification:

Enter date and grade achieved for each aspect/unit, for example 29/9 PASS

Standardisation record

Learner:			Unique learner number:	
Qualification:			Level:	
Standardising assessor:			Original assessor:	
Aspect/s of qualification standardised:				
Checklist	Yes	No	Comments/action required	
Is there an agreed appropriate assessment/action plan with SMART targets?				
Are the assessment methods fair and ethical?				
Were the methods used appropriate?				
Does the evidence meet ALL the required criteria?				
Is the evidence VACSR?				
Is there an assessment feedback record (adequate and developmental)?				
Do you agree with the assessment decision?				
Are all relevant documents signed and dated (including countersignatures if applicable)?				
Are original assessment records stored separately from the learner's work?				
Response from original assessor:				

Signed (standardising assessor):   **Date:**

Signed (original assessor):   **Date:**

Key: SMART: specific, measureable, achievable, realistic, time bound
VACSR: valid, authentic, current, sufficient, reliable

Personal development plan

Name:

Organisation:

Timescale	Aims	Costs involved/ organisational support	Start date	Review date	Completion date *CPD record to be updated*
Short term					
Medium term					
Long term					

Continuing professional development record

Name:

Organisation:

IfL number:

Date	Activity	Venue	Duration	Justification towards assessment role/ subject specialism	Further training needs	Evidence Ref Number *e.g. personal reflections, notes, certificates, etc.*

Reflective learning journal

Name: **Date:**

Experience *significant event or incident*	
Describe *who, what, when, where*	
Analyse *why, how (impact on teaching, learning and assessment)*	
Revise *changes and/or improvements required*	

APPENDIX I PRINCIPLES AND PRACTICE OF ASSESSMENT (CTLLS STANDARDS)

Level 3

Learning outcomes The learner can:	Assessment criteria The learner will:
1 Understand key concepts and principles of assessment	1.1 Identify and define the key concepts and principles of assessment
2 Understand and use different types of assessment	2.1 Explain and demonstrate how different types of assessment can be used effectively to meet the individual needs of learners
3 Understand the strengths and limitations of a range of assessment methods, including, as appropriate, those which exploit new and emerging technologies	3.1 Identify the strengths and limitations of a range of assessment methods with reference to the needs of particular learners and key concepts and principles of assessment 3.2 Use a range of assessment methods appropriately to ensure that learners produce assessment evidence that is valid, authentic, current, sufficient and reliable 3.3 Explain how peer and self-assessment can be used to promote learner involvement and personal responsibility in the assessment of their learning
4 Understand the role of feedback and questioning in the assessment of learning	4.1 Explain how feedback and questioning contributes to the assessment process 4.2 Use feedback and questioning effectively in the assessment of learning
5 Understand how to monitor, assess, record and report learner progress and achievement to meet the requirements of the learning programme and the organisation	5.1 Specify the assessment requirements and related procedures of a particular learning programme 5.2 Conduct and record assessments which meet the requirements of the learning programme and the organisation including, where appropriate, the requirements of external bodies 5.3 Communicate relevant assessment information to those with a legitimate interest in learner achievement
6 Understand how to evaluate the effectiveness of own practice	6.1 Reflect on the effectiveness of own practice taking account of the views of learners

Level 4

Learning outcomes: The learner will:	Assessment criteria The learner can:
1 Understand key concepts and principles of assessment	1.1 Summarise the key concepts and principles of assessment
2 Understand and use different types of assessment	2.1 Discuss and demonstrate how different types of assessment can be used effectively to meet the individual needs of learners
3 Understand the strengths and limitations of a range of assessment methods, including, as appropriate, those which exploit new and emerging technologies	3.1 Evaluate a range of assessment methods with reference to the needs of particular learners and key concepts and principles of assessment 3.2 Use a range of assessment methods appropriately to ensure that learners produce assessment evidence that is valid, authentic, current, sufficient and reliable 3.3 Justify the use of peer and self-assessment to promote learner involvement and personal responsibility in the assessment of their learning
4 Understand the role of feedback and questioning in the assessment of learning	4.1 Analyse how feedback and questioning contributes to the assessment process 4.2 Use feedback and questioning effectively in the assessment of learning
5 Understand how to monitor, assess, record and report learner progress and achievement to meet the requirements of the learning programme and the organisation	5.1 Review the assessment requirements and related procedures of a particular learning programme 5.2 Conduct and record assessments which meet the requirements of the learning programme and the organisation including, where appropriate, the requirements of external bodies 5.3 Communicate relevant assessment information to those with a legitimate interest in learner achievement
6 Understand how to evaluate the effectiveness of own practice	6.1 Evaluate the effectiveness of own practice taking account of the views of learners

Level 3

Learning outcomes The learner can:	Assessment criteria The learner will:
1. Understand the principles and requirements of assessment	1.1 Explain the function of assessment in learning and development 1.2 Define the key concepts and principles of assessment 1.3 Explain the responsibilities of the assessor 1.4 Identify the regulations and requirements relevant to the assessment in own area of practice
2. Understand different types of assessment method	2.1 Compare the strengths and limitations of a range of assessment methods with reference to the needs of individual learners
3. Understand how to plan assessment	3.1 Summarise key factors to consider when planning assessment 3.2 Evaluate the benefits of using a holistic approach to assessment 3.3 Explain how to plan a holistic approach to assessment 3.4 Summarise the types of risks that may be involved in assessment in own area of responsibility 3.5 Explain how to minimise risks through the planning process
4. Understand how to involve learners and others in assessment	4.1 Explain the importance of involving the learner and others in the assessment process 4.2 Summarise types of information that should be made available to learners and others involved in the assessment process 4.3 Explain how peer and self-assessment can be used effectively to promote learner involvement and personal responsibility in the assessment of learning 4.4 Explain how assessment arrangements can be adapted to meet the needs of individual learners

5. Understand how to make assessment decisions	5.1 Explain how to judge whether evidence is: • sufficient • authentic • current 5.2 Explain how to ensure that assessment decisions are: • made against specified criteria • valid • reliable • fair
6. Understand quality assurance of the assessment process	6.1 Evaluate the importance of quality assurance in the assessment process 6.2 Summarise quality assurance and standardisation procedures in own area of practice 6.3 Summarise the procedures to follow when there are disputes concerning assessment in own area of practice
7. Understand how to manage information relating to assessment	7.1 Explain the importance of following procedures for the management of information relating to assessment 7.2 Explain how feedback and questioning contribute to the assessment process
8. Understand the legal and good practice requirements in relation to assessment	8.1 Explain legal issues, policies and procedures relevant to assessment, including those for confidentiality, health, safety and welfare 8.2 Explain the contribution that technology can make to the assessment process 8.3 Evaluate requirements for equality and diversity and, where appropriate, bilingualism in relation to assessment 8.4 Explain the value of reflective practice and continuing professional development in the assessment process

Level 3

Learning outcomes The learner will:	Assessment criteria The learner can:
1. Be able to plan the assessment of occupational competence	1.1 Plan assessment of occupational competence based on the following methods: ● observation of performance in the work environment ● examining products of work ● questioning the learner ● discussing with the learner ● use of others (witness testimony) ● looking at learner statements ● recognising prior learning 1.2 Communicate the purpose, requirements and processes of assessing occupational competence to the learner 1.3 Plan the assessment of occupational competence to address learner needs and current achievements 1.4 Identify opportunities for holistic assessment
2. Be able to make assessment decisions about occupational competence	2.1 Use valid, fair and reliable assessment methods including: ● observation of performance ● examining products of work ● questioning the learner ● discussing with the learner ● use of others (witness testimony) ● looking at learner statements ● recognising prior learning 2.2 Make assessment decisions of occupational competence against specified criteria 2.3 Follow standardisation procedures 2.4 Provide feedback to learners that affirms achievement and identifies any further implications for learning, assessment and progression

3. Be able to provide required information following the assessment of occupational competence	3.1 Maintain records of the assessment of occupational competence, its outcomes and learner progress 3.2 Make assessment information available to authorised colleagues 3.3 Follow procedures to maintain the confidentiality of assessment information
4. Be able to maintain legal and good practice requirements when assessing occupational competence	4.1 Follow relevant policies, procedures and legislation for the assessment of occupational competence, including those for health, safety and welfare 4.2 Apply requirements for equality and diversity and, where appropriate, bilingualism, when assessing occupational competence 4.3 Evaluate own work in carrying out assessments of occupational competence 4.4 Maintain the currency of own expertise and competence as relevant to own role in assessing occupational competence

APPENDIX 4
UNIT 3 – ASSESS VOCATIONAL
SKILLS, KNOWLEDGE AND
UNDERSTANDING
(LEARNING AND DEVELOPMENT
STANDARDS)

Level 3

Learning outcomes The learner will:	Assessment criteria The learner can:
1. Be able to prepare assessments of vocational skills, knowledge and understanding	1.1 Select methods to assess vocational skills, knowledge and understanding which address learner needs and meet assessment requirements, including: ● assessments of the learner in simulated environments ● skills tests ● oral and written questions ● assignments ● projects ● case studies ● recognising prior learning 1.2 Prepare resources and conditions for the assessment of vocational skills, knowledge and understanding 1.3 Communicate the purpose, requirements and processes of assessment of vocational skills, knowledge and understanding to learners
2. Be able to carry out assessments of vocational skills, knowledge and understanding	2.1 Manage assessments of vocational skills, knowledge and understanding to meet assessment requirements 2.2 Provide support to learners within agreed limitations 2.3 Analyse evidence of learner achievement 2.4 Make assessment decisions relating to vocational skills, knowledge and understanding against specified criteria 2.5 Follow standardisation procedures 2.6 Provide feedback to the learner that affirms achievement and identifies any further implications for learning, assessment and progression

3. Be able to provide required information following the assessment of vocational skills, knowledge and understanding	3.1 Maintain records of the assessment of vocational skills, knowledge and understanding, its outcomes and learner progress 3.2 Make assessment information available to authorised colleagues as required 3.3 Follow procedures to maintain the confidentiality of assessment information
4. Be able to maintain legal and good practice requirements when assessing vocational skills, knowledge and understanding	4.1 Follow relevant policies, procedures and legislation relating to the assessment of vocational skills, knowledge and understanding, including those for health, safety and welfare 4.2 Apply requirements for equality and diversity and, where appropriate, bilingualism 4.3 Evaluate own work in carrying out assessments of vocational skills, knowledge and understanding 4.4 Take part in continuing professional development to ensure current expertise and competence in assessing vocational skills, knowledge and understanding

APPENDIX 5
ASSESSOR CHECKLIST

☐ Do I need to achieve the Learning and Development Assessor Units? If so, do I know who will countersign my decisions until I am qualified?

☐ Do I need to participate in any CPD?

☐ Do I have a copy of the qualification handbook and assessment strategy?

☐ Do I understand the awarding organisation requirements for the qualification?

☐ Do I attend regular team meetings?

☐ Do I have the opportunity to standardise my practice with other assessors?

☐ Does my internal quality assurer/moderator or manager need to observe my practice?

☐ Do I know who my external verifier/moderator is?

☐ Have all my learners been registered with the awarding organisation and also have a unique learner number (ULN)?

☐ Am I familiar with the Awarding Organisation's policies and procedures?

☐ Do I have an overall assessment tracking sheet for my group?

☐ Am I familiar with all the assessment records?

☐ Do I need to carry out initial assessments with my learners?

☐ Have I completed assessment plans with each learner, with suitable dates, times and assessment methods, taking into account any special assessment require-ments and health and safety aspects? Does the learner have a copy?

☐ Do I need to liaise with anyone else, for example workplace supervisors?

☐ Can I differentiate my activities to suit all my learners?

☐ Can I utilise new and emerging technologies?

☐ Do I need to produce a marking scheme with expected responses?

☐ Do I need to complete any specific records whilst assessing performance or knowledge?

☐ Do I feel confident at making assessment decisions?

☐ Did the evidence I assessed meet standards of validity, authenticity, currency, sufficiency and reliability (VACSR)?

☐ After each assessment, have I completed the feedback record and given a copy to the learner?

☐ Was my feedback positive and developmental?

☐ Do I need to review the learner's assessment plan for future or additional assessments?

☐ Do I keep copies of records in accordance with the Awarding Organisation requirements?

☐ Do I know what to do if a learner appeals against my decision?